From My Sister Carol For My 78th $6.95
Birthday 4 June 1993 which I
Spent in the Hospital

Montana Weather

compiled by
Carolyn Cunningham

D1706984

Montana Magazine, Incorporated
Helena, Montana 1982

Recipe For Cough Medicine Page 150

Second Printing, 1983

Published by Montana Magazine, Inc.
Box 5630, Helena, Montana 59604

Publisher - Rick Graetz
Editor - Mark Thompson
Managing Editor - Carolyn Cunningham

ISBN 0-938314-03-3

TABLE OF CONTENTS

Foreword 1

CHAPTER ONE - FORECASTING & MEASUREMENT
Climate Change 11
22,500 Miles High: Satellites Watch Over Montana 15
Montana's Weather-Balloon Program 17
Long-Range Weather Forecasting 20
Montana's Snow Survey 23
Farmer's Almanac 25
Is Your Thermometer Accurate? 26
Wind Chill Factor 28
Weather Observers 31
70 Below 33
Climate on the Ground 35
Montana's Coldest Spot 38
Montana's Warmest Areas 40
Cloud-Gazer's Primer 41
Types of Precipitation 47

CHAPTER TWO - RESEARCH IN THE BIG SKY
Missoula Lightning Lab 49
Fire Weather 55
Miles City Cloud-Seeding Project 60
Livingston Wind Farm 65

CHAPTER THREE - THE BIG EVENTS
Mount St. Helens & Weather 67
Winter of Calamity 1886-87 70
Weather & the Infantry at Ft. Shaw 75
Flood Years 81
    Fort Benton Fought the Missouri 85
    Milwaukee Trestle Collapse, 1938 88
    Over the Top at Gibson Dam, 1964 90
    St. Mary Deluged, 1964 92
Avalanche, Glacier's Goat Lick Slide 97
Two Unusually Severe Spring Storms 100
Waterspouts 104
Montana Twister 107
The Day Gov. Nutter's Plane Went Down 109
Great Falls' Wonderful, Winterless Winter 110

Snow Eater, Montana's Chinooks 114
Glacier Park Mini-Climate 116
Yellowstone Weather 119
Reading the Montana Skies 122

CHAPTER FOUR - MONTANA WEATHER - LIVING WITH IT

Not a Drought 'Til It Breaks Your Heart 127
Direct Hit: Lightning Plane Pilot 130
Sense and Nonsense: Weather Proverbs 131
Beyond the Comfort Range: Montana Record-Breakers 137
Weather Woes For a Montana Veterinarian 139
Surviving West Yellowstone in Winter 142
Uncle Louie's Solution to Winter 148
A Recipe for Cough Syrup & a Cure for Winter Blues 150
Author Notes 152
Glossary of Weather Terms 153

COVER PHOTO BY JOHN ALWIN

Foreword

by Warren G. Harding

Montana, the fourth largest state in the union, is a land of many climates. It is a land of mountains, plains and a combination of the two. The location of the state and its distance from the Pacific Ocean, the Gulf of Mexico, the Gulf of Alaska Low and the Great Basin High all contribute to the unique blend that is Montana weather.

There are those who deride Montana's weather and consider the state an undesirable place to live. However, in defense of our weather, anyone watching the television news stories covering the crippling blizzards of the Midwest and East, hurricanes, devastating tornadoes, floods, days and nights of extreme heat with high humidity, ice storms, dense fog that lasts for days, and mud slides, that occur over the rest of the nation, should compare what they see with our own climate. Montanans seldom abandon their automobiles under huge snowdrifts or need storm cellars to escape tornadoes. Our hot days are made bearable by low humidity and the promise of cool nights. We have never boarded our windows against hurricanes. Even our coldest winter storms are usually relieved by the chinook winds. We have suffered some losses from flooding, but in comparison with other states, they have been minor. Our greatest threat is the thunderstorm with its accompanying lightning which kills or cripples more of our people than any other weather phenomenon.

The favorable climate of Montana is the basis of the success of its largest industry, agriculture. It is also the key to the lumber industry.

Montana lies in the strong belt of westerlies which move out of the Pacific Ocean and deposit much of their precipitation on the mountain ranges of the Pacific Northwest and Montana. The mean, or average, storm track out of the semi-permanent Gulf of Alaska Low is across British Columbia and eastward across the prairie provinces of Alberta and Saskatchewan. When this weather regime is entrenched firmly over western North America, Pacific weather systems already have lost a considerable portion of their moisture on the coastal ranges before reaching Montana, and the remaining precipitation is largely confined to the mountains of the state.

Strong downslope winds sweep across the plains east of the Continental Divide with this drying weather pattern commonly called a chinook. The predominantly westerly flow is dramatically reflected in the precipitation normals for the months of October through March when the Gulf of Alaska Low is most active, and the jet stream is north of the state. Kalispell is closest to the mean storm track. It is in an "orographically" favored position. That is, because of its surrounding high mountains that give lift to the air mass, it has a precipitation normal of 7.41 inches during this six month period, while Billings, on the east slopes of the Rockies, shows a six month normal of 4.64 inches, and Glasgow, still further from the mountains, has only 2.34 inches during the same period.

1

Arctic outbreaks onto the plains east of the divide prevent further dropping of precipitation normals in the fall and winter at such locations as Billings and Glasgow. The cold dense arctic air mass forces Pacific air to rise just as it would rise over a mountain range, thus causing what little precipitation there is during October through March.

The advance or retreat of arctic air provide the much publicized temperature changes or contrasts over the plains of Montana. Cold, heavy arctic air behaves more like water than air, and the normal mixing between different air masses does not occur along the arctic ribbon or front. This results in extreme temperature gradients, both horizontally and vertically. When the artic air flows over the Continental Divide into the Flathead Valley, the cold northeasterly winds often will give more severe blizzard conditions through the passes and canyons than were present in the storm when the cold air originally moved out of the prairie provinces into Montana. The same is true when the arctic push continues through Rogers Pass, resulting in the well-known Hellgate winds and the associated blizzard conditions at Missoula.

As spring approaches, March storms are often a combination of arctic and spring type snowstorms. March can give the most severe storms of the year. Below zero temperatures are still possible along with heavy snow and strong winds.

When spring arrives, the strong westerly flow from the Pacific weakens considerably as compared to the fall and winter months. This makes the state more vulnerable to subtropical moisture; that is, moisture from the Gulf of Mexico. As the circulation of the storm systems becomes more easterly, we see a significant change. The eastern slopes of the Rockies, so dry with the westerly flow, become wet as gulf moisture reaches the state on easterly winds via the Midwest. April sets the stage for the record-breaking spring snowstorms which are so beneficial to winter wheat, spring grains and the ranges. Unfortunately they often cause considerable loss of young calves and lambs, and in some cases, full grown cattle and sheep.

This seasonal change of the storm systems from the mountains west of the divide to the plains can be illustrated by comparing the March and April normals of Summit, in the wet mountain climate of northwestern Montana, to Havre, which has a dry climate during westerly flow. Summit's March normal precipitation of 3.18 inches decreases in April to 2.93 inches, while Havre's March precipitation of .49 of an inch doubles to 1.02 inches in April, thus reflecting in their normals the increased storm activity over the plains in April and the decreasing westerly flow over the entire state.

The arrival of May continues the trend set in April. There are slow moving weather systems from the north and east, and air masses capable of carrying more moisture than those of April. The subtropical moisture is carried even further north into the prairie provinces of Canada. Thus a developing storm over the plains of Montana can receive subtropical moisture from the north, south and east, as well as Pacific moisture from the west.

By the middle of May the state is approaching its "rainy season," most pronounced east of the Continental Divide. June is the wettest month, followed by May, over most of Montana with the exception of some areas of

2

the northwest such as Summit and Trout Creek, where the wettest months are November, December and January; and northeast Montana, where July is normally wetter than May. The average rainy season is from May 20 through June 20. The wettest week of the year is usually the first week of June. In recent years there has been a trend for the rain to begin earlier and end sooner along the east slopes of the Rockies. For example, the normals now in use, based on the years 1941 through 1970, show Billings with a May total of 2.08 inches and the June normal at 2.61 inches. John Fassler, state hydrologist for the National Weather Service, reports that 30-year normals including 1981 would show May to be a wetter month than June in south-central Montana. Needless to say, if this is a long-term trend, the effect on agriculture will be important. However, this apparent trend may be only the result of some exceptionally wet storms in May.

To illustrate the importance and timeliness of the May-June precipitation east of the divide, a look at the yearly normal at Kalispell airport shows that of the 16.24 inches annual normal, 4.36 inches or 27 percent fell in May and June. At Miles City where the annual normal is 13.93 inches, the May-June normal is an impressive 5.38 inches or 39 percent of the yearly normal. Missoula with a yearly normal of 13.34 inches has a May-June normal of 3.80 inches or 28 percent of its yearly normal. On the other hand, Lewistown with a yearly normal of 17.47 inches receives 7.16 inches during May and June which is 41 percent of its yearly normal. Lewistown enjoys the distinction of having it both ways. It is located "orographically" such that it receives some precipitation from the faster moving westerly systems, as Kalispell does, and it is usually right in the middle of the large-scale storm systems east of the divide.

When winter snowpack in the mountains is abnormally low as was true at the beginning of May 1981, the onset of the rains can be a lifesaver for those dependent on snow runoff for hydroelectric power, irrigation and stock reservoirs. However, when the snowpack is normal or higher, the warm rains may give devastating runoff flooding. The snow melt is often accelerated by the long southerly flow of unseasonably warm air found ahead of many heavy rain patterns. Combined with the heavy, embedded thunderstorms so common in May and June rainstorms, the pattern for flooding is complete. The 1964 flooding both east and west of the Continental Divide from Rogers Pass northward into the southern Canadian Rockies is an example of all the necessary ingredients coming together the first week in June with the subsequent record breaking rainfall and runoff.

July and August are normally Montana's warmest months and much of the precipitation falls as showers during thunderstorms. If a weather system of any strength crosses the state, the precipitation is usually showery, with a general rain pattern quite rare. There is also a marked difference between the thunderstorms in July and August compared to those of May and June. The rainy season thunderstorms are associated with large-scale storm systems well endowed with moisture as well as strong temperature differences. The resulting heavy rains and hail can cover extensive areas of the state and often move from the east to the west, releasing torrential rains as they lift over the mountains. As the air masses become warmer and drier in July and August, the convective activity generally moves from the southwest to northeast ahead of Pacific systems, with the hail tracks tied to the topography of the state. July and August thunderstorms will be more scattered and often drier. However, they may be destructive with wind and hail. The higher bases of the clouds give "dry thunderstorms" and their accompanying vivid lightning, spectacular to viewers.

September in Montana is an obvious transition month and extremely variable. Hot weather may end abruptly during the last of August or the first part of September as a major storm sweeps the state. The first snow may fall during the first week of September, and the growing season often ends with a sharp freeze. Along the east slopes of the Rockies there is an upsurge of precipitation—a "mini" wet season, very important in the sprouting of winter wheat. This is illustrated clearly at the Livingston airport station with its August precipitation normal of 1.16 inches increasing to 1.61 inches in September, and then dropping back to 1.14 inches in October.

The October temperature and precipitation normals can be rather surprising. Its Indian summer weather is often the most pleasant of the entire year, and temperatures are usually a little warmer than April. However, a vicious fall snowstorm, much like its cousin the April snowstorm, can also sweep the state. Some years October has been the driest month of the year.

By November the annual intensification of the Gulf of Alaska Low is underway and strong southwesterly winds associated with Pacific weather systems again sweep over the divide onto the plains. Arctic air deepens over northern Canada as the days shorten. The first major arctic outbreak with below-zero temperatures may reach the plains east of the divide during November, but normally it occurs the first week of December.

The use of normals to describe the weather over Montana gives a smoothed curve of the actual changes taking place and does not picture the extremes or variations that occur. For example, some years August is wetter than June. Other years the rainy season cannot be turned off as was true in 1953 when the Highwood Mountains received more than 25 inches of precipitation in less than a month, and rain gauges along the Sun River showed more than 12 inches during the same period. The opposite occured when Belfry had only 2.97 inches of precipitation during the entire year of 1960

When studying the daily weather systems that make up the normals, a meteorologist in the field of forecasting looks at the weather differently than a climatologist. The forecaster studies each system and its effect on a given area on an individual basis, while the climatologist is more interested in the net result of a series of weather systems and how the composite will affect crops, stream flow, etc. For this reason, when zone forecasts for Montana were begun in the early 1970s by the National Weather Service, the traditional five climatic zones were further subdivided into nine forecast zones. The only change in this original map has been the moving of Deer Lodge County, which includes the city of Anaconda, from the West Central Zone to the Southwestern Zone.

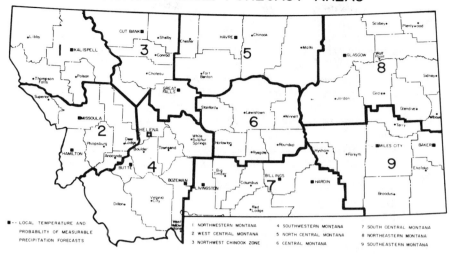

MONTANA ZONE FORECAST AREAS

■ - LOCAL TEMPERATURE AND
PROBABILITY OF MEASURABLE
PRECIPITATION FORECASTS

1 NORTHWESTERN MONTANA
2 WEST CENTRAL MONTANA
3 NORTHWEST CHINOOK ZONE

4 SOUTHWESTERN MONTANA
5 NORTH CENTRAL MONTANA
6 CENTRAL MONTANA

7 SOUTH CENTRAL MONTANA
8 NORTHEASTERN MONTANA
9 SOUTHEASTERN MONTANA

MONTANA'S WEATHER ZONES

ZONE I

Zone One, the Northwestern Zone, is the wettest. Its yearly normal is 23.03 inches and ranges from 39.22 inches at Summit to 15.66 inches at Kalispell. The precipitation is mostly supplied by Pacific moisture, although in some cases subtropical moisture does reach the zone from east of the Continental Divide during large-scale easterly storm systems. The heaviest precipitation normally falls during the months of strongest westerlies, November through Februrary. Both Whitefish and Kalispell show a May-June rainy season, but most of the precipitation data from the zone reflects the heavy winter precipitation regime.

Arctic air spills into the zone from the northeast when the cold air has deepened to 5,000 feet mean sea level (m.s.l.) along the east slopes of the Rockies from Lethbridge to Cut Bank. The combination of moist Pacific air being lifted both by the mountains and the building arctic dome can produce severe blizzard conditions in the passes and canyons.

ZONE 2

Zone Two, the West Central Zone, has the mildest winter temperatures of all the zones. Only the deepest of arctic outbreaks reach the area, spilling through Rogers Pass, or, much less frequently, pushing into the area from the north. Since stagnant wind conditions in the winter, accompanied by low clouds and fog, tend to hold down the afternoon maximum temperatures while holding up the night time minimums, Missoula's normal January temperature of 20.8 degrees is actually a little under the zone's January normal of 24.8 degrees. Some stations in the chinook belt have warmer winter normals than those of the West Central Zone, but

5

when the wind chill factor is taken into consideration, the award for the most pleasant winter climate must go to the West Central Zone where there is less wind.

The yearly precipitation normal for the zone is 15.87 inches. Although it is located west of the Continental Divide, the annual precipitation normals of many of its valley stations are little different than those east of the divide. In fact, Missoula's normal of 13.34 inches and Hamilton's 12.99 inches are both less than yearly normals of Billings and Great Falls. The strong westerlies tend to carry precipitation over the valleys, depositing the moisture on the surrounding mountains. Haugen reflects this strong orographic precipitation regime over the zone with an annual normal of 31.94 inches. The normals for May and June over the zone show a rainy season trend, although it is not as pronounced as in many areas east of the divide.

The winter storm track across southern Canada affects the West Central Zone much less than it does the Northwestern Zone. The Great Basin High over Nevada, Utah and southern Idaho, so persistent in the winter months, exerts a strong influence in holding down precipitation in the valleys. When this high breaks down and the storm track from the Pacific crosses Montana, the valleys of this zone receive their most significant precipitation.

ZONE 3

The Northwest Chinook Zone is truly the battleground of the arctic and Pacific air masses. This battle begins about the first of November and does not end until April. Looking at a relief map, the cause of all this can be seen clearly. First, the change from mountainous terrain to the plains is very abrupt from Great Falls northwestward along the Continental Divide with this same rapid drop continuing across Alberta. As the cold, dense arctic air flows southeastward across Alberta and Saskatchewan into northern Montana, its westward motion is completely halted by the Rocky Mountain Front. The arctic air will not flow up and over the divide into western Montana, but continues to deepen. As it becomes deeper, its southern push is partially blocked by the northern slopes of the Big Belts, Little Belts and the Highwood Mountains. This blocking to the south is not as unbroken as it is to the west, thus allowing the arctic air to continue its southeastward journey into south central Montana as well as into the Helena Valley.

Oscillations of the arctic front along the western foothills of this zone bring about the sharp temperature changes along a line from Great Falls to Augusta, then northward to Browning and Pincher Creek, Alberta. In fact, three national records are held along this line. At Browning on January 23 and 24, 1916, an arctic outbreak dropped the temperature from 44 degrees above zero to 56 degrees below zero in 24 hours, establishing a national record which is still unequalled. At Great Falls on January 11, 1980, the temperature rose from 32 degrees below to 15 degrees above zero in seven minutes. This information was obtained by a recording thermometer, or thermograph, and considering that a thermograph often has a slight lag when measuring such a rapid temperature shift, the change was probably even more spectacular. The third national record is shared between the Northwest Chinook and the West Central Zones at Rogers Pass. On January 20, 1954, the official temperature reading at the pass was 70 degrees below zero. This record is for the 48 contiguous states.

The zone shows a pronounced rainy season during May and June with an annual rainfall of 14.10 inches.

ZONE 4

The Southwestern Zone has the greatest variety of climates within its boundaries of any of the zones. In some respects it is a continuation of the West Central Zone although lying generally east of the Continental Divide. Many of its valleys are shielded from precipitation by surrounding mountains as shown by the yearly normal for Helena of 11.38 inches, slightly less than Havre. The Big Hole area in this zone is famous for its lush pastures and hay meadows, yet nearby Dillon airport has an annual normal of only 9.55 inches of which 41 percent or 3.90 inches falls during May and June. The yearly normal precipitation for the zone is 14.78 inches.

A "mini" chinook belt is found between Townsend and Three Forks.

The effect of the terrain on various weather systems is extremely important as to the amount of precipitation a given spot in the zone will receive. The lift of the mountains and its effect is shown dramatically by comparing the yearly normal of 13.91 inches at Belgrade with that of Bozeman where 18.66 inches fall. The Belgrade station is 10 miles from Bozeman and farther from the mountains.

The valleys of this zone show exceptionally large temperature drops at night when clear skies occur under a dominating ridge or high pressure. This is particularly true when there is a snow cover. The valleys actually produce their own arctic air mass, and under ideal radiation conditions, continue to lose more heat at night than the sun can add during the short winter day. At times Helena, Belgrade and Butte have colder minimums than Havre and Glasgow even though the latter are well entrenched in the true arctic air.

The arctic air masses from northern Montana spread across the zone, but a look at a relief map shows the difficult route the cold air has to take in order to cover it completely. It moves into the Helena Valley if a depth of 6,000 feet m.s.l. is maintained as far south as Great Falls. In order to reach Bozeman, the cold air often must deepen sufficiently in the upper Yellowstone Valley to allow it to flow through Livingston and through Bozeman Pass. To reach Butte, it may have to come in from the direction of Whitehall to the east.

The Southwestern Zone has the distinction of being the spawning area for summer thunderstorms. They develop during the afternoon over the mountains of this zone, spread northeastward and fan out with the line of greatest frequency extending from Monida Pass to Lewistown in the Central Zone.

ZONE 5

The North Central Zone represents the climatic transition from the milder winter regime of the Northwest Chinook Zone to the cold winter regime of the Northeastern Zone. The mean position of the arctic front is along the western edge of this zone, with Fort Benton having a January temperature normal of 18.8 degrees, while Malta, on the eastern edge of the zone, has a January normal of 10.9 degrees. Because the Bear Paw Mountains and the Little Rockies act as a southern barrier to arctic outbreaks, there are dramatic temperature contrasts along the north slopes of these mountains. If there were more reporting stations in the area to record these contrasts, they would rival the records of the Northwest Chinook Zone. While Havre, Chinook, Harlem and Malta are shivering in below zero weather, ranchers from the Bear Paws and Little Rockies often come into town and tell of thawing temperatures and "water running everywhere." Before Bull Hook Creek was rerouted from the center of Havre to the east, chinook winds sometimes melted heavy snow in the Bear Paw Mountains and the hills surrounding Havre, causing a rapid runoff into the creek and flooding of the streets. When the arctic air pushed back into town, the water froze curb to curb, providing excellent ice skating.

The zone has an annual normal of 11.73 inches and is the driest of the zones. The precipitation normals are quite uniform along the Milk River with Havre, Chinook, Harlem, Turner and Malta all having annual normals from 11.50 inches to 12 inches. Fort Benton, located in the southwest corner of the zone, has a higher rainy season normal which brings its yearly normal to 14.78 inches. The Bear Paw Mountains, the Little Rocky Mountains and the Sweet Grass Hills all have considerably more precipitation than the towns at lower elevations.

ZONE 6

The Central Zone is characterized by its topography which wrings moisture out of Pacific systems in a westerly flow pattern and Canadian systems in a northwesterly to northeasterly flow pattern. It is similar to the Northwest Chinook Zone with strong southwesterly winds sweeping the zone from time to time during the fall and winter months. Arctic air sweeps quite easily across the zone from the north, and the funneling of cold air between the Little Belt Mountains and the Big Snowy Mountains often gives extreme blizzard conditions from Stanford through Judith Gap to Harlowton, with stranded motorists not uncommon.

The zone has an average yearly precipitation of 14.10 inches. Normals range from 17.47 inches at Lewistown down to 11.64 inches at Roundup. The Central Zone has a high frequency of thunderstorms during the summer months due to its own topography and its downstream position from the thunderstorm spawning mountains of southwestern Montana and the upper Yellowstone Valley. These thunderstorms are often accompanied by severe hail with the Judith Basin area among the hardest hit.

ZONE 7

The South Central Zone has within its boundaries the highest mountain of the state, Granite Peak, with an elevation of 12,799 feet, one of the many high mountains in the Beartooth range, on the southern border of the state. The mountainous terrain of the southern and western sections of this zone provides upslope lift for Pacific weather systems, causing them to release significant amounts of their precipitation. However, the lift on northeasterly winds, the flow so often involved in spring storms as well as the rainy season pattern, is much more important in giving the zone an annual normal of 15.87 inches, second only to the Northwest Zone. It is exceeded only by our Southeast Zone in availability of sub-tropical moisture from the Gulf of Mexico. The zone exhibits a pronounced rainy season pattern. Livingston airport has a May-June normal of 5.23 inches.

The arctic outbreaks often lose momentum after crossing the Central Zone and move into the South Central Zone much weaker and shallower. At times the arctic front will become stationary west of Billings and never reach the Livingston area

The southwesterly wind regime from Livingston to Big Timber during the late fall and winter months is one of the strongest observed along the east slopes of the Rockies. It is difficult to say whether it exceeds its rival, the East Glacier-Browning pair.

Due to the high mountains over the western and southern portions of the zone, severe thunderstorms occur over the region. The downstream position of Billings relative to the Beartooth and Absaroka Range has given that city several devastating hailstorms during the past 50 years.

ZONE 8

The Northeastern Zone has the coldest winter temperatures. Being fur-thest from the chinook belt, the warming winds reach this area last and are less frequent. By studying January normal temperatures at stations with the same northern latitude but with increasing distance from the mean position of the chinook belt, we find Cut Bank with a January nor-mal of 16.2 degrees; Havre, 11.9 degrees; and Medicine Lake, northeast of Poplar, 7.9 degrees. Westby, being the farthest north in the Northeastern Zone and also the farthest from the chinook source, has the lowest January normal of all the recording stations, 5.7 degrees. The arctic out-breaks into Montana from Canada often reach this area first and grip the region the longest.

Summer brings a dramatic temperature reversal as the zone heats up. On the extreme side, the highest Montana temperature record of 117 degrees is shared by two stations in the zone; Glendive on July 20, 1893, and Medicine Lake on July 5, 1937.

Thunderstorms reach the zone much later in the day than those of the zones to the west. Often they begin during late evening and continue until daybreak. Due to Midwest summer moisture, this zone and the Southeast-ern Zone are more apt to have a threat of a tornado with their thunder-storms.

The zone has a normal annual precipitation of 13.36 inches. The Glasgow yearly normal of 10.87 inches is the lowest of the region and is not representative of the zone in general. Most significant is the July precipitation over the zone, with many stations having a normal ex-ceeding two inches, making it the wettest region of the state during July. Many areas of the state receive less than half this amount.

ZONE 9

The ninth zone, the Southeastern, does not reflect its proximity to Midwest moisture and storm systems in its normals of precipitation as much as one would expect. It should have a considerably higher annual normal, but lack of good upslope terrain allows easterly winds to pass over the area without releasing their moisture. As these moisture-laden winds continue westward and reach higher elevations, the precipitation increases. For this reason, during easterly winds, the probability of rain or snow at Billings is much greater than at Miles City. The zone has an annual normal of 13.92 inches and a well pronounced May-June rainy season.

During the summer months the collision of Pacific frontal systems with warm moist Midwest air masses can cause severe thunderstorms accompanied by hail. The thunderstorms occur over the zone later than those to the west, often beginning during late afternoon and evening hours and continuing well into night. The zone carries a greater threat of tornadoes in thunderstorms than do zones to the west.

Although arctic outbreaks in winter may be severe and long lasting, as a rule they are more shallow than those over the North Central and Northeastern zones and are of shorter duration. Some of the most severe winter and spring storms are associated with intense low centers over northwestern South Dakota, placing the zone in the northwest quadrant of its circulation.

Broadus has a yearly normal of 14.05 inches and receives 5.36 inches during May and June. Colstrip has a yearly normal of 15.79 inches with 5.78 inches falling during May and June.

The annual mean temperature for the state of Montana is 43 degrees, and the annual precipitation normal is 15.10 inches.

FORECASTING & MEASUREMENT

Climate Change:
A Few Degrees
Between Us and an Ice Age

by Grayson Cordell

The winter of 1780-81 was a bitter one for the American Revolutionary troops under George Washington. The poorly fed and clothed soldiers huddled around campfires at Morristown, N.J., barely able to survive the cold while the British troops remained warm in New York City a few miles away. But the British also had their troubles because the winter was so cold that parts of New York harbor froze for weeks at a time preventing movement of the British fleet. The ice even became thick enough so that cannons were hauled from Manhattan to Staten Island.

The early American settlers had struggled against extremely bitter winters ever since the colonies were settled. They did not realize it, but they were conquering the New World during some of the worst weather in more than 2,000 years. They were in the midst of a world-wide cold spell that began in the early 15th century and continued to about 1850. This period of time is known as the Little Ice Age to climatologists today.

By contrast the first half of this century was warm, the weather excellent for agriculture, and as a result the world's population doubled. We have come to accept this as our "normal" weather, but actually it is highly abnormal. In this century the world has experienced the warmest weather in the last 1,000 years. In fact, only five percent of the time during the last two million years have the earth's temperatures been as warm as this century's. This has been established by the study of fossil remains of such things as pollens, oceanic organisms and other climate-sensitive life forms.

After millions of years of tropical temperatures the earth began to cool very gradually about 50 million years ago. Approximately two million years ago the global climate suddenly changed and began a pattern characterized by the advances and retreats of massive continental ice sheets. Estimates are that there have been about 20 ice ages in the last two million years with warm interglacial periods between.

The last ice age began about 70,000 years ago. The ice sheet reached its maximum size 20,000 years ago covering North America as far south as the present course of the Missouri River. Frozen tundra extended further south. Other regions also were affected, as the great quantities of water stored in the ice sheets lowered the levels of the oceans. The glaciers began to retreat 15,000 years ago.

After the Little Ice Age ended, the world's temperatures began to rise rapidly about 1880, and this warming continued until 1940. World temperatures rose two degrees. Cooling began in the 1940s with temperatures cooling 1.1 degrees since that time. This warming and cooling may not seem like much, but estimates are that temperatures need to cool only five to 10 degrees to start an ice age. Presence of the ice sheets, once they begin to form, would then cause further cooling.

Few responsible people are predicting an ice age. However just the possibility of cooler temperatures does cause concern for agriculture and the world's ability to feed its population. This century's weather has been remarkably good for agriculture and any change is likely to have an adverse affect on food production.

World-wide warm and cool periods appear to be normal occurrences, but the warming and cooling is not evenly distributed. As the world's temperatures rose two degrees from 1880 to 1940, Norway's temperatures rose 10 degrees. Iceland is currently cooling at three times the rate of the rest of the world.

Causes of the warm and cool cycles are not known; neither are all the effects. People who study climate changes do agree on one thing though; cooler temperatures cause an increase in the variability of the weather. Alternating extremes in temperatures and precipitation in any given area would occur—more hot and cold spells, droughts and floods. This almost certainly would lower average crop yields.

The reason for increased variability is that during warm periods the circulation in the upper atmosphere is more from west to east in the temperate zones of the northern hemisphere. This results in a more evenly distributed pattern of weather varying relatively little from month to month and from season to season.

During cooler climatic periods the winds are broken into more irregular patterns by the presence of more pressure systems—both highs and lows. This causes an increase in northerly and southerly winds. The pressure systems would be more prone to stagnate over large areas for months at a time. Cold temperatures are associated with northerly winds, while unseasonably warm temperatures occur on the other side of the pressure system where southerly winds dominate. Droughts and floods become more frequent. Thus, while the hemisphere as a whole becomes cooler, individual areas may alternately break heat, cold, drought and moisture records.

The cooling would not be spread evenly. Some believe that the interior sections of the U.S. and Canada, and Europe as well, would likely cool more rapidly. In the 1930s the Midwest was seven degrees cooler than at present with northerly winds occurring much more of the time. These areas are prime breadbaskets of the world, growing large surplus crops. In contrast, it is also thought that the Ukraine may benefit from increased moist southerly flow. The political implications of Russia producing more grain while we produce less are obvious.

If further cooling should continue, effects would be more drastic. In a matter of centuries ice packs would build, without melting during the summers. Changes in vegetation would occur more quickly. Generally speaking, due to a decrease in world-wide precipitation, forests would become prairies in less than a century. Semi-arid areas like those of eastern Montana would become deserts in a few decades.

What have been the effects of the present cooling trend? During the first half of this century, when temperatures were warming, glaciers world-wide receded rapidly. In recent years some have begun growing again. Cooler temperatures now threaten the existence of some crops in Iceland. In England the growing season (time between the last front in spring and the first in the fall) has shortened two weeks in the last 30 years. The arctic ice field grew 12 percent from 1968-73, but has decreased somewhat since. Fishing off Iceland and Greenland has been affected. Warmth-loving animals in Europe and North America have been shifting their ranges southward. Hardwood forests in North America have been advancing southward.

Parts of Africa experienced severe and prolonged droughts in the 1970s. Changes in the atmospheric circulation affected the yearly monsoon seasons in some countries that are dependent upon them. Droughts hit India in the 1970s due to failure of the monsoons to return on time. Russia had repeated crop failures which affected world trade.

In our country two of the last three winters have been very severe. The summer of 1980 was extremely hot and dry in the southern and central states, as a strong high pressure system settled over much of the country, while cool weather was the rule in the Northwest.

Little planning has been done for future cooler times. It has been assumed that this century's warm weather will continue indefinitely, but history proves otherwise. Some believe that pollution of the atmosphere may be aiding the cooling trend, while others believe that the increase of carbon dioxide in the atmosphere from the burning of fossil fuels will cause further warming. At best, it is likely only to delay the next cold period. But those who study climate believe that some planning should be done for cooler times. The advantage to New Yorkers of being able to drive across a frozen harbor to Staten Island would definitely be outweighed by the miserable cold such a freeze would require!

●　　●　　●

Let's look at what has happened to Montana's weather during this worldwide cooling period.

Using rather simple statistical methods, we find that temperatures have changed very little if the entire state is considered. When different sections of the state are examined, slight warming generally is found in the west and a little cooling found in the east, but both the warming and cooling are only by several tenths of a degree.

However, the warming and cooling are not the same in all locations. In the east, Ekalaka cooled by less than half a degree, while in south central Montana, Big Timber's annual average temperature decreased by more than a degree. Townsend, near Helena, warmed by one and a half degrees.

Looking at the decades, the 1940 temperatures were nearly average in western Montana and warm in the east. The 1950s were cool and the 1960s warm throughout the entire state. Despite recent cold winters, the 1970s, when considered as a whole, had nearly average temperatures in the west, and were slightly cooler than normal in the east.

In western Montana, Thompson Falls and Cut Bank have experienced virtually no change in the average length of their growing seasons, whereas in the east, Ekalaka's growing season has decreased by more than a week.

The 1940s were slightly on the wet side; the 1950s were dry in southern Montana and wet in the north. The last 20 years have seen drier than average weather except that the 1970s were wet along the eastern slopes of the Rockies in the central sections of the state.

During the past 40 years precipitation at Big Timber and Cut Bank has shown a tendency to be slightly on the increase. Helena has seen no change and Kalispell has decreased slightly. The northeastern section of the state has experienced the greatest change, where annual precipitation has decreased by more than an inch at Glasgow.

Snowfall at Glasgow has decreased slightly—less than two inches a year. Kalispell's snowfall has increased slightly while Helena's annual snowfall trend is an increase of approximately 10 inches, with about half of this increase coming during April. West Yellowstone's snowfall has increased by more than two feet. Statewide, the 1940s had the least snow and the 1950s the most.

The 1940s also registered the least number of days of snow on the ground, with the 1950s receiving the most. The overall trend is for the number of days of snow cover to increase slightly at Helena, but only about two days a year. The continuous snow cover at West Yellowstone shows an increase of about two weeks a winter.

Throughout central Montana in recent years, not only has the appearance of chinooks been less frequent, but they've also been more brief. This allows the snow cover to remain longer.

Great Falls lies in the middle of this chinook belt. The absence of chinooks in the winter of 1977-78 caused the ground to remain snow covered for 83 consecutive days—a significant record. The following winter, snow covered the ground for 118 consecutive days, breaking the previous winter's record by a wide margin.

Helena lies outside what is normally considered the chinook belt, but still experiences the warm snow-melting winds fairly frequently. In the winter of 1949-50 snow remained on the ground in Helena for 94 consecutive days. This broke 70 years of records, only to do so again in 1978-79, when snow covered the ground for 118 consecutive days. It is also interesting to note that the length of time Canyon Ferry Reservoir near Helena remains ice covered has increased a week since the dam was constructed in the early 1950s. Fort Peck Reservoir does not exhibit this tendency. Its ice cover has remained about constant.

14

22,500 Miles High: Satellites Watch Over Montana

by William A. Rammer

It wasn't so long ago that weathermen had to depend primarily on ground-based observation of cloud formations in making their forecasts. But that all changed in 1964 with the launching of Nimbus, a satellite equipped with video cameras. Every 24 hours, the on-board cloud sensors scanned the globe twice. Set in a polar orbit, it crossed the North and South Poles, making one revolution every 98 minutes. Nimbus, or "rain cloud," passed over Montana shortly after noon (MST) and again shortly after midnight during each 24-hour period.

At 600 miles above the earth, the cameras viewed cloud and land features, relaying high quality video signals to receivers at Great Falls and elsewhere around the world. In fact, Great Falls received these signals mere seconds after Nimbus's scan of the northern Rocky Mountain area. Hard-copy photographs were then produced from the satellite information. As midnight arrived and Nimbus again passed over Montana, an infra-red sensor transmitted the cloud field pattern by converting cloud-top temperatures to visual impressions.

For the first time, weathermen in Montana could see the organized cloud patterns which might affect our weather. These patterns could then be correlated with ground observations as well as with weather-balloon measurements. However, weathermen received cloud pictures of their area only twice daily. What they really needed was a satellite in stationary orbit which could constantly scan Montana and North America as well as the surrounding ocean areas.

Thus, the Applications Technology Satellites, ATS-1 & 2, were launched in 1966. At an altitude of 22,500 miles over the equator, one at 75 degrees west longitude and the other at 150 degrees west longitude, these satellites hurtled at 6,843 miles per hour, just fast enough to match the speed of the rotating earth while maintaining altitude. This kept the satellites looking down at the same area of earth 24 hours per day in an orbit described as earth synchronous, geo-synchronous or geo-stationary. The TV camera aboard the western-most satellite took pictures of North America and the Pacific Ocean every 30 minutes. At night, infra-red sensors were used to get cloud pictures, as with the Nimbus system.

At this point, meteorologists had the tool to make high quality analyses of cloud and weather systems on a continuous basis. Motion of cloud systems could be observed by stacking several hours of photographs (two each hour) and then thumbing through them to get a kaleidoscopic effect. State and national boundaries, latitude/longitude lines as well as other topographic features were inscribed on each photograph by a computer-photo process before development, so that the weatherman could determine the location on earth of the cloud fields.

Pictures from this geo-stationary satellite led to some improvement in the forecast process, particularly in the short-range period of less than 12 hours. The greatest use was for timing of cloud fields associated with cold fronts or upper troughs as they approach Montana, particularly if no change occurs in the character or intensity of the associated weather system. Unfortunately these weather satellite systems were given advanced billing as being the ultimate solution to the weather forecast problem. It was suggested that perfect forecasts would be prepared for one to two weeks into the future. This proved to be overly optimistic since the forecaster continues to struggle, at times, to make *tomorrows's* forecast perfect.

Satellite cloud pictures do have shortcomings. For instance, rain or snow areas cannot always be determined from the picture alone, but only through verification by a ground-based observer. In addition, the cloud picture does not indicate the height above ground of the base of the cloud layer, which is essential for aviation weather forecasting. Most importantly for Montana, the pictures do not indicate well enough in advance where and when large-scale storm development will occur. The relationship between various cloud-pattern signatures and major storm development is much more evident over the uniform, moist ocean areas than over the rough terrain of North America. The recent deployment of a satellite weather camera which views moisture patterns even in the absence of

Figure 1

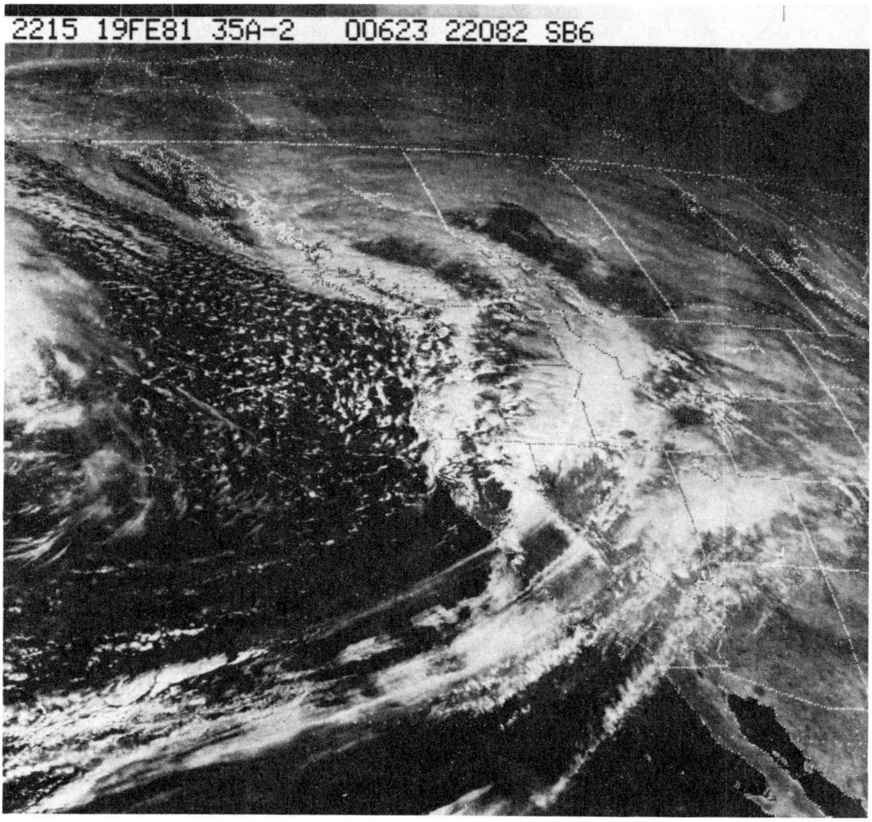

2215 19FE81 35A-2   00623 22082 SB6

clouds will offer an opportunity for more complete diagnosis of weather systems particularly over continental areas.

Figure 1 shows a typical satellite picture from a geo-stationary orbiting camera. The legend at the top of the picture indicates that the picture was taken at 2245 Greenwich Mean Time or 4:15 pm MST of the 19th of February, 1981. The arcing cloud pattern from western Montana to southern California delineates a cold-frontal cloud system moving from west to east. The small, cigar shaped clouds just northeast of Canyon Ferry reservoir in the Helena area are lenticular clouds which indicate southwesterly downslope wind flow from off the Rocky Mountains. This flow also is characterized by the relatively clear area (dark colored) over most of southwest and southern Alberta, caused by air sinking after crossing the Rockies; as it becomes warmer and less humid and therefore, more cloud-free, the Montana chinook can sometimes result.

The cold air mass behind the cold front extends westward to well offshore of Oregon and Washington. Cold air over relatively warm ocean water produces an unstable condition, causing "boiling" motions in the lower atmosphere. Cumuliform-type clouds, identified in this picture by the large, speckled area west of Washington and Oregon, are produced. Thin cirrus clouds from the next approaching weather system are moving onto the west-central border of the picture. One rare aspect of this particular shot is the presence of the moon above the darkened area of the earth in the upper right corner. This picture was provided by the National Environmental Satellite Service and the National Weather Service.

Journey to the Stratosphere: Montana's Weather-Balloon Program

by Warren G. Harding

Twice daily at approximately 4 a.m. and p.m. (MST) an unusual sight may be seen at both Great Falls and Glasgow. A large hydrogen-filled balloon is released to begin its journey to the stratosphere carrying the equipment to make the rawinsonde (upper air sounding) observation. This balloon and its train rise at the approximate rate of 1,000 feet per minute, and as it ascends, the attached radio transmitter sends the pressure, temperature and humidity of the air through which it is passing back to the ground recorder. By means of tracking devices, wind speed and direction are also calculated.

While the two stations in Montana are taking their observations, the same operation is being performed at stations all over the world, using similar instruments, reporting the same data in the same codes so the information will be available to all meteorologists on a global basis. The basic rules and regulations under which the program is carried out are decided by the World Meteorological Organization, with each country responsible for the operation of its own segment.

F O R E C A S T I N G & M E A S U R E M E N T

The balloon is filled with hydrogen generated at the station. For many years weather stations in the United States used helium from mines in Amarillo, Texas to fill all weather balloons. The supply is now diminished and with the increased cost of transporting the 120 pound cylinders of compressed helium, its use has become impractical. A filled balloon prior to release is shaped like a tear drop, about 12 feet tall and approximately six feet at its widest point. As it ascends, it expands due to the decreasing pressure of the atmosphere. When it reaches its ultimate height at about 25 miles, the balloon, now approximately 50 feet in diameter, will burst. Tied between the balloon and transmitter is a parachute which opens after the balloon bursts, allowing the transmitter to float back to earth instead of plummeting as it otherwise would.

The release of the balloon and its train on a calm, warm day is usually uneventful and routine. However, the same operation, when strong winds and precipitation are present, especially at night, can be harrowing, and first attempts may not be successful. Although the balloons are quite durable, with a heavier type available for use during severe weather, they are not indestructable, and occasionally strong wind gusts will cause breakage during the attempt to remove them from the inflation shelter. A large balloon filled with hydrogen exerts considerable force, and combined with a strong wind, can be like a wild animal struggling to escape its captor. Some stations are relatively free of obstacles which hinder release, but light poles, fences, snowdrifts and even parked vehicles may cause problems. Placing a delicate instrument on the end of the train adds to the problem of achieving a successful release.

Once the launch has been completed, the instrument is tracked by a directional finding antenna, similar to radar equipment. With radar the signal is sent out by the antenna on the ground and then reflected back to earth by the object being tracked. This method was originally tried in rawinsonde observations, but because of snow and other precipitation interference, the signal was cluttered and the method rejected. By using the directional finding method, the antenna homes in on the signal emitted from the instrument, and, once fixed on the signal, rarely loses it.

As the balloon and its train ascend, the wind usually carries them outward from the release point, and the landing site is often many miles away. Wind currents have been known to carry them far from the station during the first part of the flight, while changing air currents at higher levels return them close to the release point. In one rare instance, the instrument was found within one mile of the station. All instruments are labeled with the point of origin plus date and time of release, and instructions to return to the weather service. A small portion of the total instrument is reusable.

The signal which transmits the data is picked up on the ground by a special receiver, where an observer and a computer prepare the information for transmission to all weather offices. The finished product gives a cross section of the atmosphere from the surface of the earth into the stratosphere. These reports are gathered from all over the world and fed into computer centers such as the National Meteorological Center near Washington, D.C. With this information, forecasts of the movement of the atmosphere for 96 hours are made. It is the basis of forecasts made by the weather service meteorologists, as well as military, private and television weather specialists. Without it, the forecasts of today would be impossible.

Following World War II one remarkable weather ship remained in service in the Gulf of Alaska. It was originally nicknamed "Ship Papa," owned by the Canadian government and partially financed by the United States. Its position in the Gulf was permanent at 50 degrees north latitude and 145 degrees west longitude—putting it about 1000 miles west of Vancouver, B.C. and 800 miles south of Anchorage. The skill and dedication of the weathermen on this ship were remarkable considering the extreme weather systems into which they launched their balloons, as well as living on the ship 24 hours a day. Unfortunately, due to lack of funds, this ship was decommissioned June 1981, with a great net loss of information.

In nearby states, rawinsonde stations are found in Spokane, Washington; Boise, Idaho; Lander, Wyoming; Rapid City, South Dakota; Bismarck, North Dakota; and Edmonton, Alberta.

Long-Range Weather Forecasting and Other Games of Chance

by Grayson Cordell

Weather forecasts may be categorized into four classes: (1) detailed and highly accurate forecasts for the next six to 12 hours based upon radar and satellite data; (2) forecasts for tomorrow and the next day or two based upon computer products and the forecaster's experience; (3) five-to 30 day general forecasts using computer and statistical techniques plus forecaster experience and (4) long-range forecasts of several months.

However, science has not developed an accurate method of long-range weather prediction, even in a general way. There is a great need for such forecasts. Some rank this need as great as the need for a cancer cure. Unfortunately, like cancer, where science has not developed enough to produce the needed results, the door is open for unethical opportunists to take advantage of the need and to sell useless cancer cures and long-range weather forecasts to the public.

According to the National Academy of Science and the American Meteorological Society, forecasts are feasible most of the time for from one to three days, and occasionally out to five days. Beyond five days, predictions of average temperature and precipitation for periods of up to a month are of some use. Season forecasts of average temperatures for three-month periods may be valuable in a general way. Forecasts of average precipitation beyond a month are worthless. Therefore, when a forecast of a big storm is heard for a specific day next week or sometime

20

next month, you should know that it is not based upon sound meteorological principles.

Most of us have heard or seen such long-range forecasts and some of
them have been correct; forecasts, no matter how they are made, will
always be correct part of the time. A forecast that is always wrong would
require just as much skill to produce as a completely correct forecast.

Len Smallman of the National Weather Service Regional Office in Salt
Lake City did the following two experiments. The study of long-term
weather records (climatology) shows that in January there are, on the
average, six clear days, seven partly cloudy, eight cloudy, six with rain or
light snow and four days with significant snow. In November, he took 31
slips of paper, one for each day of the month, and labeled six of them clear,
seven partly cloudy, eight cloudy, six precipitation and four snow. The
employees in the personnel office then drew the slips from a hat with the
first slip drawn being the "forecast" for January 1, the second slip the
forecast for the 2nd, etc.

How did the office staff do? January that year turned out to be a wet
month having 14 days of precipitation including four days with significant
snow. The staff correctly forecast the weather 10 out of 31 days and was
correct in forecasting two of the heavier snows. If you allow them a leeway
of plus or minus one day, since the forecast was made two months in advance, they correctly forecast eight of the 14 precipitation events and hit
three of the four heavier snows—pretty good forecasting! Two young
meteorologists in the office did the same thing. Their results were not as
good, but they still were correct eight of the 31 days.

Extending the time period, Salt Lake City was in a drought at the time
and in late February a well-known opportunist from another state made a
precipitation forecast by month for the rest of the year which was publicized by a TV station. The staff went to work again having been intrigued
by the first results.

This time they used five slips of paper and a die. The slips were labeled
above normal, slightly above, normal, slightly below, and below normal.
The slips were then drawn, the first being assigned the number one on the
die, the second number two, etc. The die was rolled for each month and
the corresponding forecast written on the slip was made. Sixes didn't
count. At the end of the year both forecasts were verified. The
results—their forecast beat the opportunist's.

My point is this: Do not be deceived by the occasional hit of a long-range
forecast. Even no-skill forecasts made only by random chance are correct
some of the time.

If you believe that these experiments are a valid test showing that long-
range forecasts require no skill, then what is a person to do who wants to
take the weather into account in planning next season's business or activities? You could hire just about anybody to make you a forecast or you
could roll the die yourself. But a better solution would be the use of clima-
tological relationships. That is, using past weather records that give indi-
cations of future weather conditions.

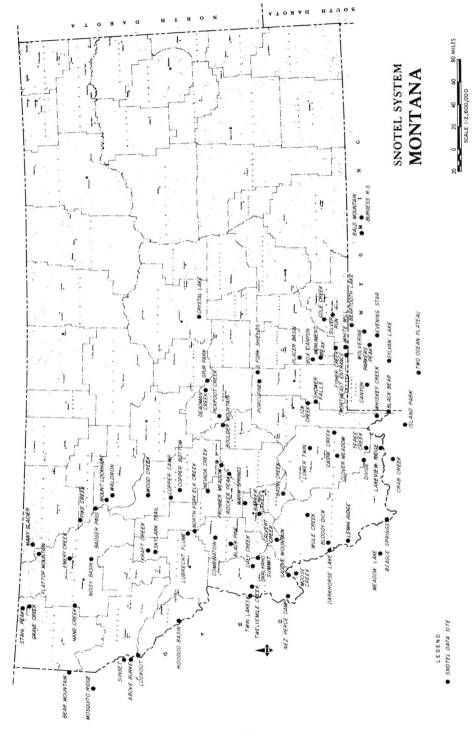

SNOTEL SYSTEM
MONTANA

SCALE 1:2,600,000

20   0   20   40   60   80 MILES

LEGEND

● SNOTEL DATA SITE

22

Montana's Snow Survey

by Phil Farnes

About 70 percent of Montana's streamflow comes from melting snow. An accurate measurement of the water content in the snowpack is an important index for predicting spring and summer runoff. The science of snow surveying began in the early 1900s above Lake Tahoe on the Nevada-California border. These first scientific snow measurements were used to predict the rise of Lake Tahoe and to end the long water war between shore homeowners and downstream irigators.

Other areas soon were making their own surveys. The first measurements in Montana were made at four locations in Glacier Park in 1922. Recognizing a need for coordination between states, Congress assigned the U.S. Soil Conservation Service to establish and coordinate a snow survey network in the western states.

In Montana, the SCS coordinates a snow survey program that involves over 25 federal, state and private agencies. The SCS and these cooperators measure the water content of the snow at 250 snow courses—official snow measuring locations. Every month from January through June, snow surveyors ski, snowshoe, snowmobile, or sometimes fly to remote mountain snowpacks to collect and report their findings. These areas, typically small meadows, are about 300 to 1,000 feet long with 10 sampling stations 25 to 100 feet apart. It is important these courses be located carefully so they are not disturbed by drifting snow patterns, ponded water or by man's activities.

PHOTO COURTESY OF SOIL CONSERVATION SERVICE

Manual equipment consists of sections of aluminum tubing that can be screwed together and pushed down to the base of the snow. An inch scale on the outside of the tube measures depth, which may be more than 20 feet. A serrated steel blade on the lowest tube is used to cut through ice layers. A calibrated scale (one ounce of snow core equals one inch of water) is also part of the surveyor's equipment. By subtracting the weight of the empty tube, he can figure water content of the core sample.

However, snow surveys are evolving from manual measurements once a month to automated snow courses that report daily. In 1963 the first remote snow sensors were installed in Montana. Now there are 65 remote locations transmitting data on snowpack, precipitation and temperature twice daily. These automated locations are called SNOTEL (snow telemetry) sites. They use a new kind of communications that reflect signals from meteor trails. The data from the remote sites is transmitted to one of two master stations in either Boise, Idaho or Ogden, Utah. These masters send the data to Portland where it is then returned to the interested states and other users.

Snow survey data from these snow courses and SNOTEL sites, and forecasts of expected streamflow for over 80 stream-gauging locations, are published monthly, January through June, in the Water Supply Outlook for Montana. Irrigators and reservoir operators are the big users of snow survey information. From the monthly reports, they can gauge the availability of water for irrigating nearly two million acres of land in Montana. Streamflow forecasts are used for evaluating flood potential, hydroelectric power generation, water quality, low flows, sediment transport, impact on fisheries, recreation and wildlife.

Basic snow survey data is used for calculating snowloads, total snowfall, average annual precipitation at higher elevations, adequacy of snowfall at potential ski areas, evaluating wintering stress on wildlife, avalanche hazard, natural variations in annual snowfall and long-range snowfall trends, and a host of other relationships and indexes.

The snow survey program will continue to change as water becomes more costly, water users increase and new technology becomes available.

The SCS plans to install additional automated sites for two reasons. The first is to obtain a more complete coverage of the state's snow resource areas. The second reason is to make snowfall, snowpack, precipitation and temperature data available on a real-time basis from most remote areas. Eventually, the automated sites will become part of the data base for daily forecasting of weather, runoff and numerous other conditions related to mountain climate.

An extensive network of automated sites will also allow streamflow forecasts to be issued on a daily basis during critical time periods in addition to the seasonal runoff periods.

Manual snow measurements will be phased out as soon as SNOTEL data is correlated with historic data.

Management of water supplies will become more critical as users increase. Snow survey data will become more valuable to those making decisions that affect Montana's precious and bountiful water supply.

Farmer's Almanac: Can You Believe It?

by Grayson Cordell

The need for long-range weather forecasts often prompts folks to rely on questionable information. The oldest and probably most frequently quoted forecast of this doubtful type is found in the Old Farmer's Almanac.

The Almanac predicted a mild mid-January in 1982 for the east and south sections of the country, but these areas actually shivered under record cold. Although the Farmer's Almanac could have made a chance mistake, recent study by two weather researchers seems to indicate that the Almanac has a consistent record of poor forecasts. One could do almost as well by blind guessing.

The Almanac's forecasting methods are neither conventional nor well documented. The publication carries this statement: "Our forecasts are determined both by the use of a secret weather-forecasting formula derived by the founder of this almanac in 1792 and by the most modern scientific calculations based on solar activity." Whatever the methods, results differ little from flipping a coin, according to John Walsh and David Allen.

These two men are research meteorologists at the University of Illinois at Urbana. They conducted a study comparing five years of the Almanac's forecasts with the weather that actually occurred. This was done partially in response to some local farmers' high regard for the Almanac. No matter what the accuracy, the Almanac definitely has its faithful followers.

The weather records in 32 cities were used to verify the weather in the Almanac's 16 forecast regions. Miles City was one of the cities used. Forecasts were compared to the weather that actually occurred.

According to Weatherwise magazine the forecasts for above or below normal temperatures were correct 51 percent of the time, for precipitation, 52 percent. To put this in the proper perspective, flipping a coin would produce the correct forecast 50 percent of the time.

The statistical analysis shows that the mean correlation between predicted and actual temperatures for the entire country was .016; for precipitation the correlation was .041. If all forecasts had been perfect, which in all fairness the Almanac never claimed, the correlations would have a value of 1.00. Random guessing produces a correlation of zero; the Almanac's predictions are only slightly more dependable.

A point commonly forgotten is that all forecasts, scientific or not, have correct results part of the time. It would take just as much skill to produce 100 percent inaccurate forecasts as to be entirely correct all of the time.

More accurate long-range weather forecasts are made by the National Weather Service, but they are not made as far in advance. Their monthly and seasonal temperature forecasts are correct approximately 60 percent year-round. Forecasts of precipitation are correct only 55 percent of the time.

Walsh and Allen also checked to see if the Almanac is correctly forecasting extreme weather such as droughts, wet spells or the unusually cold winters experienced in recent years. Twelve periods of extreme weather were compared to the Almanac's forecasts and in only three cases was even the *type* of abnormal weather predicted. In no case did the forecasts give a hint at the severity of the actual weather.

In a recent issue of Science Magazine, Jud Hale, editor of the Almanac, claims that its most accurate forecast is the one-page, essay-style national forecast. But he also readily admits that this forecast is too generalized and subjective to be verified statistically.

Is Your Thermometer Accurate?

by Grayson Cordell

It is not uncommon for your home thermometer to register a different temperature than the official reading given on the local radio or television station. Yet, at other times it agrees. Is there something wrong with your thermometer? How can you tell?

There are times when your thermometer should give about the same reading as the official temperature. At other times, different readings are appropriate.

If it is windy and your thermometer is located approximately at the same elevation as the National Weather Service or Federal Aeronautics Administration (FAA) office where the official temperature is recorded (usually the airport), then both temperatures will be about the same. The same is also true if it has been cloudy for a long time although temperatures will vary a little more. But on clear and calm nights, the varied terrains of Montana cause wide variations in temperature over short distances. These natural variations are even more pronounced if the ground is snow covered.

On these clear and calm nights, cold air drifts downhill in the same manner as water. The coldest air settles in the lowest areas. Thus, it is a natural phenomenon that the valley floor is colder at night than the surrounding hillsides, and such temperature differences are more pronounced in winter when the nights are long.

Valley temperature variation can be very large, especially when the snow is deep. For example, Helena's airport is located at the southern edge of a somewhat circular valley with the town setting on the hillsides just to the southwest. The lowest part of the valley lies to the north. At night, during the cold season, it is common for the upper part of Helena to be up to 15 degrees warmer than the airport while the lower portions of the valley may dip from 10 to 15 degrees colder. Thus, temperature differences of 30 degrees are possible between locations in Helena and parts of the valley.

The airports in Great Falls, Billings, Lewistown and Dillon are located on plateaus above town, so under similar conditions the towns will record colder temperatures than the airports.

Elaborate precautions are taken by the National Weather Service to minimize outside influences in its efforts to measure the true temperature of the air in the shade at a height of about five feet. So any thing that has an effect on your thermometer will cause an inaccurate reading.

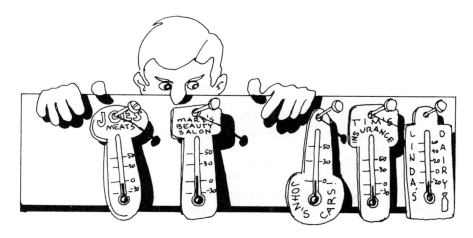

Direct sunshine will affect your reading of course, but sunlight can also be reflected by nearby objects such as a neighboring house. Thermometers can receive heat through your window or door. If temperatures are below zero, every little influence will throw off the reading. Even the heat from your body as you approach will cause the mercury to rise a few degrees.

If you think your thermometer is off, its accuracy can be checked easily. First, check to see if there are any breaks in the glass or the mercury or alcohol column. If there are, discard it.

If there are no breaks, then crush some ice or use snow. Put the ice or snow in a glass (a small thermos bottle is more accurate) until the ice starts melting. A small amount of water can be added initially to speed up the melting. Put the thermometer in the melting ice and let it sit so it can reach an equilibrium condition. The temperature of melting ice is 32 degrees and that is what your thermometer should read. If it doesn't, you can apply a correction to your readings in the future.

Your correction should be determined so that the final figure is 32 degrees. If your thermometer reads 35 degrees, your correction is minus three degrees. If you read 30 degrees, then add two degrees to your readings in the future. If your readings are more than a few degrees off, you probably should get a new thermometer.

Wind Chill Factor—How Fast You Freeze

by Grayson Cordell

Air temperature is not always a reliable indicator of how cold one may feel. Perception of cold is affected by "wind chill," a measurement of quality which was first developed in 1939 by Dr. Paul Siple, who accompanied Admiral Byrd to the Antarctic. Siple's later work there, along with the findings of Charles Possel as well as the U.S. Army during and after World War II, is an index of the air's cooling power. The wind chill index is based on the idea that coldness is related to the loss of heat from exposed flesh. This rate of heat loss can be measured.

During the Antarctic winter of 1941, Siple and Possel discovered how long it took a given amount of water in a plastic container to freeze under a variety of wind and temperature conditions. The results were plotted against wind speed and a general formula for heat loss was derived.

The formula measured the cooling power of the wind and temperature in complete shade. Although it does not consider all the methods by which the body can lose heat, it does give a good measure of the *air's* ability to carry heat away from the body.

How chilly a person feels also depends on factors other than the wind and temperature. Humid air transfers heat away from the body slightly faster than dry air. Precipitation on the skin, either rain or snow, increases heat loss. The body also loses heat by contact with cold objects. Sitting on the ground, or especially a rock, accelerates this loss. A considerable amount of body heat is lost from the lungs when cold air is breathed—the colder the air, the greater the heat loss.

Of course, an individual's metabolism, the state of nourishment and the state of health also have effects. Poor circulation will cause a person to feel colder, because the body does not generate heat as rapidly as someone in good health. The slower blood circulation impairs the process of replacing heat loss from the skin and extremities with heat from the body's interior. Protective clothing is the only method we have of combatting the cold outdoors. During physical exertion, the body's heat production increases, but perspiration causes part of this additional heat to be lost by evaporation. Perspiration also causes dampness in protective clothing, and the insulation qualities of the cloth are decreased.

The wind chill index also does not account for any heat gained from sunshine. A considerable amount of heat is generated even in the middle of winter, especially if the ground is snow covered. Fresh snow on an open field reflects up to 9 percent of the incoming sunlight. Thus there is an abundance of sunlight to be absorbed by any dark object, and a person

WIND CHILL FACTOR

Equivalent Temperature (°F)

Calm	35	30	25	20	15	10	5	0	-5	-10	-15	-20	-25	-30	-35	-40	-45
5	33	27	21	16	12	7	1	-6	-11	-15	-20	-26	-31	-35	-41	-47	-54
10	21	16	9	2	-2	-9	-15	-22	-27	-31	-38	-45	-52	-58	-64	-70	-77
15	16	11	1	-6	-11	-18	-25	-33	-40	-45	-51	-60	-65	-70	-78	-85	-90
20	12	3	-4	-9	-17	-24	-32	-40	-46	-52	-60	-68	-76	-81	-88	-96	-103
25	7	0	-7	-15	-22	-29	-37	-45	-52	-58	-67	-75	-83	-89	-96	-104	-112
30	5	-2	-11	-18	-26	-33	-41	-49	-56	-63	-70	-78	-87	-94	-101	-109	-117
35	3	-4	-13	-20	-27	-35	-43	-52	-60	-67	-72	-83	-90	-98	-105	-113	-123
40	1	-4	-15	-22	-29	-36	-45	-54	-62	-69	-76	-87	-94	-101	-107	-116	-128
45	1	-6	-17	-24	-31	-38	-46	-54	-63	-70	-78	-87	-94	-101	-108	-118	-128
50	0	-7	-17	-24	-31	-38	-47	-56	-63	-70	-79	-88	-96	-103	-110	-120	-128

(Windspeed — Miles per hour. Embedded zones: VERY COLD, BITTER COLD, EXTREME COLD)

Read right and down from calm-air line. For example, a calm-air temperature of zero degrees Fahrenheit (0°F) has an equivalent cooling effect of minus 40°F at a wind speed of 20 miles per hour.

walking in a field will receive a great deal more heat than if the ground were free of snow.

A common question is: If the temperature is 30 degrees and the wind chill index is about 10 degrees, will an exposed object take on the temperature of the air or that of the wind chill index? The answer is the temperature of the air, not of the index, for objects cannot become colder than the air itself. However, objects will cool faster and reach the temperature of the air more quickly than if no wind is blowing. The wind-chill index is an attempt to indicate how quickly the object will cool to the air's temperature; in this case, as fast as if the air were 10 degrees with no wind.

The Wind Chill Equivalent Table provided by the National Oceanic and Atmospheric Administration gives equivalent temperatures for various combinations of wind and temperature. An example from the table shows that a temperature of 30 degrees and a wind speed of 15 m.p.h. has the same cooling power as a temperature of nine degrees and wind speed of four m.p.h. Four m.p.h. is usually used as a base for tables because that is approximately the speed of an adult walking briskly. Wind speeds greater than 40 m.p.h. have little additional cooling effects.

It has been found that, depending upon other factors previously mentioned, freezing of flesh begins at about 20 degrees below zero equivalent temperature. At an equivalent temperature of near minus 70 degrees, an unprotected face will freeze in less than a minute; in less than 30 seconds at minus 90 degrees.

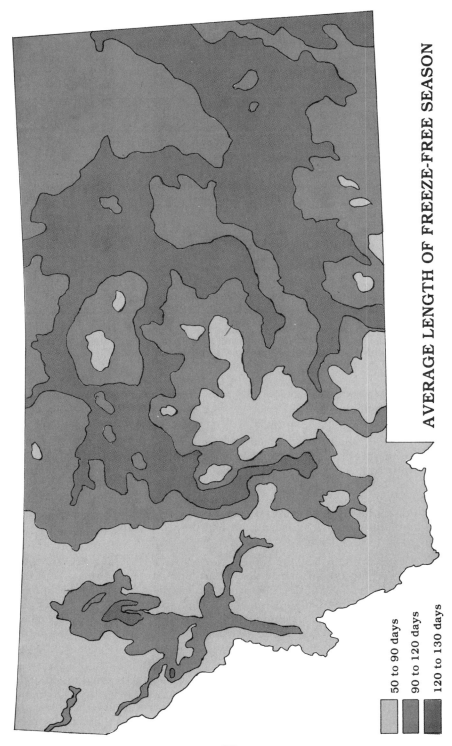

AVERAGE LENGTH OF FREEZE-FREE SEASON

50 to 90 days
90 to 120 days
120 to 130 days

Weather Watchers Network

by Grace D. Harding

Present day scientists who wish to learn of the climate in centuries past must study tree rings, rock formations, soil samples, high and low water marks, and traces of vegetation. Their conclusions, although assumed to be reasonably correct, can never be verified. However, future generations with an interest in what happened climatically in the United States during the twentieth century will have a wealth of detailed data to study. This collection of information is the result of the efforts of a dedicated group of people known as the "Cooperative Observers."

These folks have been designated by the National Weather Service to keep a daily record of the maximum and minimum temperatures, precipitation, and snowfall, plus any pertinent weather phenomena which occur. The equipment used is furnished and maintained by the weather service, but the observer provides services free of charge. The reward is the satisfaction of keeping valuable records and being part of a network of people with a common bond.

There are approximately 380 cooperative observers in Montana. When these stations were established, the goal was to have an observation site every 25 miles, but with the many square miles of mountains and sparsely populated prairies of Montana this has been impossible, Nevertheless, all sections of the state are represented in the network.

The data from the collected observations are invaluable. All climatic normals are established by these records, with 30 continuous years necessary before a normal can be determined. Only by studying the statistics thus gathered can a true picture of Montana's weather be obtained.

At the end of each month, the observers mail their records to specified collection points, one being the National Climatic Center at Asheville, North Carolina, which is the location of the archives for the nation's weather data. During the period from April 1 to October 31, approximately five percent of the observers are designated to report a weekly summary of their observations by telephone to the National Weather Service state forecast office at Great Falls. This material is forwarded to the statistical reporting office of the United States Department of Agriculture at Helena, where it is used in the weekly crop report for the nation. It is also used in the computation of the Palmer Drought Index and the crop moisture index which are of vital concern to the agricultural segment of the country.

From April 1 to September 30, approximately 10 percent of the observers telephone the weather service office when their stations receive one-half inch or more of precipitation. This is vital information used in the forecasting of flooding. Other observers record and report the heights of streams.

Cooperative observer status often becomes a family tradition, with sons or daughters taking over the responsibility when a parent wishes to be relieved of the duty. Occasionally it is taken over by a neighbor, but when there is no such volunteer, an advertisement in the nearest newspaper or the post office usually brings forth someone who wants to take part.

Five observers have been singled out for their extraordinary service over many years by having received the Montana Television Network Jefferson Award: *Frank Cimrhakl, Jr., Roy; Mary F. Harker, Heron; Edwin E. James, Cascade; Andrew Johannsen, Dunkirk; Mr. and Mrs. Ira Vinion, Fort Benton.*

Behind the Statistics: A Weather Observer's Reminiscence

by Mrs. Ruth Cameron

The Weather Station was simply "Cameron, Meagher Co., State of Montana. Observer, Lewis Cameron, Sr." Recordings began on June 1, 1909. For the next 16 years he never missed a day recording weather observations. That first day there was no precipitation, an east wind, clear sky. Just an ordinary day, as were the hundreds that followed.

But behind statistics there are always stories. There was March 25, 1912 when his grandson Harry was born half a mile away. He didn't record that, just the 26.0 inches of snow on the ground, cloudy with an east wind. That grandson, incidentally, became my husband many years later.

Or another date. November 29, 1918, a trace of snow on the ground, northwest wind, cloudy. That was the day he got the telegram informing him his youngest son, George, age 27, had died in France on November 1. More than four years later, on January 4, 1922 George's body was laid to rest in the White Sulphur Springs cemetery. A clear day. 8.0 inches of snow, high temperature of 34.

He started recording temperatures in 1912, the same year the station become Findon. That was the name of the new post office established in his home, named for his birthplace in Scotland.

Those first three years were severe winters with snow coming in mid-November and piling up steadily to over 30 inches by February, and no bare ground until April.

He didn't often make remarks in the column reserved for them, but extremes did get attention. In June of 1913 he said he "had not seen so many thunder storms in one month in the 22 years I have been in the state."

In January, 1916, a month of very cold temperatures reaching to 37 below (the lowest he ever recorded) brought the comment that the "wheat probably survived due to deep snow and the stock were in remarkably good condition." On May 25 of that year he remarked " 7 a.m. 4 inches of snow." I think he was tired of it. October that year drew another sentence.

"Storm of 1, 2 and 3 the most severe storm on record at this station in the month of October." It totaled only 10 inches of snow but had temperatures in the low 20s and fierce wind.

1917 began with an accumulation of snow from December, 1916 of 19.7 inches and it kept getting deeper. 35.2 inches by the end of January and 51.1 inches at the last of February. March stayed cold and the snow stayed on, 47 inches by the 30th. By April 30 he had had it. There were still 31 inches on the ground. "Spring work way behind. No plowing done and not likely to be any. Snow storms on the 15th and 25th through 29th the worst I have ever seen in April. Loss of stock must be heavy."

The summers of 1915, 1920 and 1923 must have been great for growing of crops and terrible for harvesting. Precipitation averaged around three or more inches a month May through September. But the winter of 1920 was exceptionally dry. In February he recorded, "There has been no hand feeding of stock all winter and grass is turning green." By March 12th it was 10 below. No comment from the observer.

The summer of 1919 was a scorcher with highs of 91 and 93 every month June through September. The highest temperature in those 16 years was 96 degrees in July, 1921.

He ended his observer years on June 30, 1925 with this: "On the 27th, two distinct earthquake shocks, one at 6:26, the other at 7:10 p.m. Each lasted a few seconds. My house trembled and dishes rattled." That was the quake that devastated Sixteen Mile Canyon many miles away.

He was 72 years old and getting tired. In 1933 he died a few months after I married his grandson. In 1937 I began keeping weather records at the old Findon Post Office but gave it up in 1942 to move away for school. The equipment was moved 11 miles to Martinsdale where Mrs. Grace Coates kept the station until 1963 when I again took it over, this time five miles from Martinsdale where I still live. I keep records yet but not with the faithfulness of Lewis Sr. I miss a day or more now and then. Still there is a fairly complete record for this area for 72 years.

70 Below and Maybe Lower

by Grayson Cordell

Snow had been falling almost continuously for a week in the Montana Rockies. It was cold, very cold; the temperature had only risen to minus 18 degrees. Finally, late in the day, the snow and wind stopped, skies cleared rapidly, and as the sun set the temperature plummeted. Early the next morning on Jan. 20, 1954, Montana's and the continental 48 states' record cold temperature of minus 70 degrees was observed at a mining camp near the Continental Divide a short distance from Rogers Pass near Helena.

The record temperature was observed by one of the National Weather Service's (formerly the U.S. Weather Bureau) cooperative observers.

PHOTO BY RICK GRAETZ

The Rogers Pass weather station was established May 1, 1953, at the 4 K's Mine located at Highway 200 and three-fourths of a mile west of where the highway crosses Rogers Pass. The mine was located at an elevation of 5,470 feet above sea level.

At the time, the mine was being developed by three brothers and a nephew, the Kleinschmidts. The nephew, H.M. Kleinschmidt, was listed as the official observer, but all four were interested in the weather station. A Weather Bureau record made at the time the station was established says: "...At present they are just digging the tunnel and haven't reached the ore yet. So it is hard to tell whether they will be there long or not. If the ore vein is good it would be for many years."

The minus 70 degree temperature occurred on Jan. 20, 1954, but Richard A. Dightman, State Climatologist at the Weather Bureau, was not aware of it until about February 3 when January's records were received at the Helena office. The January 20 minimum temperature was entered as minus 68 degrees. Dightman noticed that this would be a record, if valid, breaking the old national record of minus 66 degrees at West Yellowstone, Montana, on Feb. 9, 1933. So Kleinschmidt was contacted and asked to send in his thermometer to be checked and to provide any other information he could to help evaluate the reading.

He not only sent in the official minimum thermometer, but also included his own alcohol thermometer. He wrote that he was awake most of the severely cold night because of loud and frequent "popping" noises in the cabin. About 2 a.m. he got up and looked at his thermometer located outside an insulated window. It read about minus 68 degrees. He then went outside to the official shelter and found the minimum thermometer indicating a temperature colder than minus 65 which is as low as the scale on it indicates. The minimum index from which the temperature is read had retreated into the bulb and was tilted since the index end had fallen into the bulb.

The two thermometers were sent to the Weather Bureau's Instrument Division in Washington, D.C. where they were checked in the laboratory exactly as the observer described. The index in the official thermometer fell into the bulb and remained at the described angle at a temperature of minus 69.7 degrees and at this temperature, Kleinschmidt's personal thermometer indicated minus 68 degrees.

Conditions had been right for an extreme temperature. The station was located at a high elevation in a saucer shaped depression. During the previous week there were several fresh invasions of very cold arctic air into Montana. Seven days of almost continuous snow increased the snow depth from eight inches to 66 inches at the mine. The night was crystal clear with no wind—ideal conditions for strong cooling.

Perhaps it should be pointed out that the record is an extreme occurring in an extreme location under extreme conditions—in a small, high mountain valley with 5½ feet of snow on the ground, 58 inches of which had fallen recently. The minus 70 degree reading was not representative of the more densely populated areas of the state; that night a low of minus 31 degrees occurred in Butte, minus 43 degrees in Havre, minus 34 degrees in Billings, minus 37 degrees in Great Falls, minus 36 degrees in Helena and minus 14 degrees in Missoula.

The facts that the two thermometers behaved in the laboratory exactly as described by the observer, that temperatures of minus 57 degrees and minus 59 degrees were recorded in the same general area and that the observer was not aware that he was recording a record temperature were sufficient evidence to adopt the minus 70 degree record.

Most stations are supplied with thermometers similar to Kleinschmidt's that only go to minus 65 degrees. Thus, these thermometers cannot break the record. We know only that on that night it was *at least* minus 70 degrees; it very well may have gotten colder but the thermometer was unable to record it. The minus 70 degree reading was at 2 a.m. and normally the night's minimum temperature occurs shortly after sunrise.

The record more than likely will have to be broken in a high mountain valley somewhere in Montana or perhaps Wyoming. A few selected weather stations in areas such as this are supplied with colder reading thermometers.

And not only must the extreme conditions *exist* to establish a new record, but someone has to be there to observe!

Our Brutal Climate on the Ground

by Grayson Cordell

It was a pleasant late summer day with a high temperature of 75 degrees after an early morning low of 40 degrees and a brief but heavy afternoon shower. These "official" temperatures were taken at a height of about five feet above the ground. Years of observations have shown that at this height, influences on the temperature by nearby objects, the condition of the ground below, and the vegetation growing on it have largely been eliminated. It is thus representative of the surrounding area.

These temperatures are then experienced where people live; they are representative of the human climate. But what kind of a day was it below this height; especially in the first few inches above the ground in what is known as the "microclimate?"

As one approaches the ground, the climate becomes substantially different. It becomes more extreme and varies greatly over very short distances, for the nearer the ground, the more the wind speed is reduced by friction with the ground. Thus, the mixing of air is greatly reduced and it is this mixing that reduces the differences in climate among small areas.

During the day the atmosphere is largely heated from below—by the ground which is heated by absorbing the sun's energy. However, the ground is not heated evenly, for the type of soil, its dryness, and the amount and type of vegetation covering it influence how much of the sun's heat it absorbs. On a sunny day, the drier the soil, the more loosely packed it is, the larger the soil particles (sand vs. clay), the less the vegetative cover, the hotter the soil surface. This in turn causes the air just above it to be hotter.

At night the atmosphere is cooled by contact with the earth below. The same conditions causing hotter soils during the day cause colder conditions at night. And the greatly decreased wind speeds in the microclimate cause large temperature differences over short distances, perhaps only a few feet.

The microclimate of bare soils is hotter in the day and colder at night than grassy fields. Hot temperatures near the ground bend light rays causing the mirages often seen in the desert or on highways. Ground under a thick forest cover experiences the smallest temperature fluctuations between day and night.

Why are we interested in the microclimate? To the meteorologist this is the boundary layer between the earth and the atmosphere, a knowledge of which is necessary to understand the larger processes taking place in the atmosphere. It is in the microclimate that plants grow, especially young plants that are very susceptible to weather fluctuations. Unwinged insects live here as do the small animals that must live on or near the ground.

A knowledge of happenings in this layer near the ground is helpful to people interested in plants and animals; the farmers, foresters, gardeners, botanists, zoologists and others. Even people interested in the state of the ground; traffic engineers, water and soil experts, geographers and architects.

Much can be learned about a large area by study of the weather statistics, but deductions about the microclimate cannot be made from these figures. For example, during one particular May in a large city only one night of frost was experienced, with a low temperature of 29 degrees. Outside the city, 10 miles away, frost occurred a few inches above the ground on 23 nights during the month. Temperatures dropped to as low as 6 degrees.

Even the slightest slope of the ground has an influence, as it affects the angle of sunlight striking it. Southern slopes, of course, receive the most solar energy and are therefore much warmer than northern slopes.

Land sloping to the east warms faster in the morning than western slopes, but the mid-afternoon summer sun is less intense. The uneven melting of snow on calm, clear days is indicative of the sun's intensity on various slopes.

The colder the air the more dense it becomes. Therefore, at night, the air cooled by contact with the ground flows downhill like water and collects in low places. Hence, valleys experience lower nighttime temperatures than surrounding hillsides. The coldest temperatures usually occur in the lowest part of the valley.

Farming in Montana is basically of the dry-land type. There is plenty of heat available during the summer for the growing of grains; the question is whether or not there will be enough rain.

But the growing of vegetables, such as tomatoes and cucumbers, is a different matter. For successful growth, the warmest spot available should be chosen.

For the successful growing of crops in marginal climates, the slope of the land is again important. For example, in Germany rainfall is plentiful, but heat is somewhat lacking. Vineyards are quite successfully grown on terraces on southern slopes where the most heat is available.

In other parts of the world plenty of heat is available, but water is scarce. In these areas the shady northern slopes are preferred since evaporation is less. In the Sinai Peninsula the skimpy vegetation that does grow is found on the northern slopes.

Much of the world's fruit, and especially that grown in this country, is grown in marginal climates, that is, in climates where spring frosts occur at least occasionally. Many fruit orchards in these regions are on hillsides where the occurrence of frost is less frequent. It only takes one cold night in the spring to ruin a crop and damage or destroy the fruit trees.

If a very cold night does occur and a general frost is expected, frost preventive measures are easier and usually more successful on slopes. This is because even if frost occurs, the layer of cold air is not as deep as in the lower areas.

Cloudy or windy weather decreases the microclimate effect. Clouds serve as a blanket, greatly reducing the buildup of heat or cold near the ground, and wind disperses the day's heat or nighttime cold.

The mountain winter snowpack protects young vegetation from winter's icy storms and gives warmth to the small creatures near or below the ground. Beneath the snowpack the ground is not frozen. Even if the ground freezes in early winter due to a lack of snow, it quickly thaws from the heat that is transmitted from deep in the ground after deep and insulating snows arrive.

But just above the snow pack on the ridges and other windy areas a hostile climate exists. The winter winds lift ice particles from the snowpack, smashing them against all objects. This "sandblasting" effect damages or kills the limbs of trees within a foot or two of the snow. It is very difficult for young trees to force their way up through this hostile zone in exposed areas.

Tree damage is easily recognized. The low limbs that lie beneath the winter snowpack are long and full. Above these limbs will be an area perhaps a couple of feet long where there are no limbs, or at least none on the west side of the tree, and the bark will be quite scarred. Above this the tree has normal growth.

The microclimate has an effect on a larger scale also. The movement of valley and mountain breezes is a good example.

Cold air seeks lower levels, warm air rises. After sunset, if the sky is relatively clear and the winds light, the ground cools quickly and then cools the air above. This cool air then moves down the mountainside, then down the valley. This mountain drainage breeze is easily seen in the evening by simply watching the smoke of a campfire. The opposite effect takes place after heating begins the next morning.

A knowledge of these breezes can be helpful to the hunter. By looking at a mountainside at dawn on a clear and calm morning, the hunter can plan a strategy. Shortly after sunrise, uphill breezes will begin carrying the hunter's scent ahead of him if he climbs in a sunny area, but downhill breezes will continue for quite a while on the shady side of the mountain or in shady draws.

By mid-day, air currents will be rising. Later, as the sun falls behind the mountain, downhill breezes will begin on the shady east side of a ridge while they continue to rise on the sunny sides of the mountain.

On a windy day these breezes are overpowered by larger weather systems. Strong winds disperse the hunter's scent much more quickly, because the scent is mixed vertically in the air by turbulence. Under light winds the hunter's scent is trapped near the ground enabling animals to smell him at greater distances.

• • •

So what kind of a late summer day was it near the ground? Although the minimum temperature was measured at 40 degrees, there was frost in many places during the early morning.

The afternoon was pleasant near the shade of a bush. But a field mouse experienced as much temperature change as he scurried across an open patch of sand as a human experiences on a hot summer afternoon in going from an air conditioned building into the boiling sun.

To us the brief shower was refreshing and needed. To the insects and other little creatures it quickly became a flash flood.

Montana's Coldest Spot: Not West Yellowstone
by Grayson Cordell

What is the coldest place in Montana? Most people probably would answer, West Yellowstone. Some may even be of the opinion that it is the coldest place in the nation outside of Alaska. What do the weather records show?

There is no doubt that whenever cold air from the far north covers all of Montana it is the high valleys of southwestern Montana that catch the news headlines due to their extremely low temperatures. The high elevation and heavy snowcover in these valleys allow heat to escape rapidly on clear cold nights.

GREAT FALLS TRIBUNE

Survival Certificate

This Certifies that *Mira C Vinion*

has survived Montana's record cold spell — December 1968 to March 1969

I WAS THERE DURING THE WORST WINTER IN MONTANA HISTORY . . .

- A record consecutive 13 days and 14 hours, -10° or colder, January 17 through January 31, 1969.
- Record cold day in Great Falls December 29, 1968 -43°.
- Record continuous snow cover from December 19, 1968 to March 18, 1969.
- During 84 days, December 19, 1968 to March 12, 1969, 68 days 32° or colder and 20 days 0° or colder.

Mira Vinion, weather observer at Ft. Benton shares this reminder of winters passed. Montana's suffered worse since then.

The high valleys around Yellowstone Park and the Big Hole Valley are known for extremely low temperatures. In most winters the temperature will approach or exceed readings of 50 degrees below zero at least once.

If average yearly temperatures are considered, Cooke City edges out West Yellowstone as the coldest place in the state. Wisdom, in the Big Hole Valley, is the third coldest. In winter, West Yellowstone is actually the coldest, but its summers are warmer than Cooke City and Wisdom. Cooke City's cool summers give it the dubious honor of being Montana's coldest town year round.

But what if only winter temperatures are considered? Do these high valleys also have the coldest winters in the state? No!

Western Montana is frequently visited by relatively warm maritime air from the Pacific Ocean during winter. These periods of mild weather last for days or even weeks at a time. Chinook winds blow along the eastern slopes of the Rockies and extend their thawing effects out onto the plains. But the farther one is from the mountains, the less frequent these thaws.

In winter these warm winds seldom reach the eastern-most portion of northeastern Montana. Thus, all of the plains north of the Milk River and east of Malta experience the coldest winters. In this area, the further east and north one goes, the colder the average winter.

Just south of the Canadian border and just west of North Dakota, the small town of Westby must claim Montana's coldest winters. Their January temperatures average 5.7 degrees; about 6 degrees colder than West Yellowstone.

Westby's summers are much warmer than those of the cool southwestern valleys. July's temperatures average 10 degrees higher than West Yellowstone.

During December, in an average winter, Westby becomes the state's coldest town and remains so through February. Temperatures begin to rise quickly during March.

Colder winters are encountered to the east of Westby along the Canadian border in North Dakota. The extreme northeast corner of North Dakota experiences the coldest winters in the lower 48 states. In this area, January temperatures average slightly below zero. Although Westby has Montana's coldest winters, there are colder places.

Montana's Warmest Areas

by Grayson Cordell

Montana's warmest places measured by average temperature throughout the year are not necessarily the same places we think of as Montana's hottest places. Of course, the east slope of the Rockies is one of the warmer areas of the state, especially in winter, as a result of frequent chinook winds. However, Thompson Falls, on the lower Clark Fork River in extreme western Montana, is ever so slightly warmer on a yearly basis.

Big Timber on the Yellowstone River east of Livingston and Holter Dam on the Missouri River southwest of Great Falls tie for being the warmest spots in the chinook belt. But Thompson Falls' average annual temperature is one tenth of a degree warmer making it Montana's warmest town that has maintained a long-term weather record.

In winter, Thompson Falls is also the warmest town, edging out Big Timber again by only one tenth of a degree. Even though the mild chinook winds blow frequently during the winter along the Rocky Mountains' eastern slopes, very cold arctic air from the far north does invade the area on a number of occasions. These cold spells may last a few days or a few weeks.

The majority of these cold spells enter Montana over the plains, and the cold usually does not become deep enough to move westward across the Continental Divide. In some cases the cold air becomes deep enough to move into the valleys just to the west of the divide, but will not cover all of western Montana. Only a few are strong enough to cover all of the state. Thus, the farther west, the less frequent are extreme cold spells.

Thompson Falls is about as far west as one can get in Montana, and invasions of air from the arctic are probably as infrequent there as any place in the state. Relatively mild air from the Pacific covers the area most of the winter, bringing cloudiness or fog which helps to keep nighttime temperatures from dropping very much. Great temperature changes are not nearly as common as in the chinook belt. The fairly constant winter temperatures of Thompson Falls result in slightly warmer average temperatures than the widely fluctuating temperatures experienced in the chinook area.

In summer, the warmest temperatures shift eastward to the plains. Hot air originating from the Gulf of Mexico moves northward over the hot plains of the Midwest, frequently ending in eastern Montana. The common presence of the hot air coupled with the lower elevations of the plains causes this area to have Montana's hottest summers.

All of the eastern plains are warm with most of the area experiencing 40 to 50 days a summer when the temperature reaches 90 degrees or more. The Yellowstone Valley from east of Billings downstream is a little warmer than the surrounding plains on each side of the river.

Glendive is the state's warmest town during the summer months, followed closely by Miles City. During July, Miles City is actually slightly warmer. Forsyth is third.

Low-hanging stratus during a fall storm in the Bitterroot Valley. PHOTO BY TOM DIETRICH.

Cloud-Gazer's Primer
by Grace D. Harding

Montana boasts some lavishly beautiful sunrises and sunsets, and the admiring sky-gazer may not realize that our cloud formations are largely responsible for these vibrant displays.

Clouds are like people in that no two are alike. There are many different factors that determine a cloud's characteristics, and entire books have been written on the subject. Temperature, moisture, location, movement horizontally as well as vertically, and the seasons with the changing length of days are to be considered, as well as various laws of physics which need not concern the casual observer.

41

Upper: Lightning flashes within a cumulus cloud. Lower: A cumulus, or thunderhead, has risen to great heights, flattening into an "anvil cloud" as it reaches the stratosphere.

If someone were to ask a schoolboy in Kansas to describe a cloud, he would probably choose a beautiful white, billowing, clearly defined cloud with a clear blue sky accentuating its rounded top. He would be describing a cumulus congestus. The son of a fisherman in the Pacific Northwest would likely describe a cloud as grey, formed in a more or less continuous sheet with no sharp edges to distinguish it from the sky behind it. He would be describing a stratus fractus.

42

Upper: Cirrus clouds, high and wispy, may foretell an approaching storm. Lower: Multi-layered standing lenticular. A stationary wave cloud formed as strong winds blow over a mountain range. PHOTOS BY TOM DIETRICH.

These common clouds are just two of the 27 cloud types classified and recognized world wide by meteorologists and weather observers. This international system is essentially the same as the original classification done almost 200 years ago by Luke Howard, an English pharmacist. The names are Latin and have Latin meaning. Only specialists in the meteorological field concern themselves with all of these types. A casual observer of clouds can easily identify most clouds with a little basic knowledge.

There are four fundamental types of clouds containing a total number of 27 identified according to variations in their state of development, their height, and the amount present. The four that are important to know are as follows given with the Latin meaning:

Stratus: Covering. Derived from the Latin word *sternere*, to spread, stretch out, extend. A simple stratus definition in English is a low-level cloud spreading over the face of the sky, uniform and featureless.

Cumulus: A heap structure in convex masses piled one upon another. In English, a detached, dense cloud with marked vertical development. The upper surface is domelike while the base is nearly horizontal.

Cirrus: A lock, curl, tendril. Detached clouds composed of delicate white fibers and appearing in either tufts, streaks, trails, feather plumes, or bands. Often has fibrous appearance resembling carded wool. Always very high.

Nimbus: A rain cloud, a storm. A nimbus cloud is always associated with stratus, called nimbostratus, with rain falling from it. Very dark grey and thick.

Following the four fundamental classifications of clouds, the next division is the one of height. Any cloud below 6,500 feet is called a low cloud, a cloud whose base is between 6,500 and 23,000 is a middle cloud, and those above 23,000 are high clouds. The most spectacular cloud of all, the cumulonimbus, a well-developed thunderstorm type will generally have a base below 6,500 feet but will climb as it grows to heights of 60,000 feet, with its top well into the stratosphere.

A simple stratus cloud is generally a low cloud whose base can be the ground (where it is considered fog) or reach to the limit of 6,500 feet. The same type of stratus will also exist in the middle cloud bracket, but it is given a new name, altostratus, with the word alto derived from the Latin word meaning high. Stratus formed over 23,000 feet are called cirrostratus.

With cumulus clouds the same guidelines are used. A simple cumulus is found below 6,500 feet, the middle height cumulus are called altocumulus, and the high cumulus are cirrocumulus. All cirrus clouds are high and composed of ice crystals.

The heights are somewhat arbitrary. Ice crystal clouds, cirrus, form at lower elevations over the arctic region than over the tropics, and adjustments are required from pole to equator. However, the heights are guidelines and satisfactory for classification. Observers who live in mountainous areas can judge the cloud base heights by comparing them to the terrain. It is naturally more difficult on flat plains to estimate cloud heights. Pilots can give an amateur help with this.

All types of clouds can be seen in all parts of Montana. However, since the climate and geography of the state vary considerably from east to west, some are more common in one area than in another. Clouds also vary from season to season, with the huge cumulonimbus more commonly seen in the summer than any other time.

We all make mini-clouds as we go through the day; the steam in the bathroom after a shower, the steam from a teakettle, and the breath that we see when we exhale on a frosty day are all manifestations of the same phenomena. Very simply it is just a case of warm moist air coming in contact with cooler air.

In order to understand the elementary processes of cloud formation, some basic knowledge is necessary. All air contains some moisture or water vapor, invisible to the human eye, with warm air capable of holding more moisture than cold. When the air at a given temperature contains all of the moisture possible, it is said to be saturated, and the relative humidity will be 100 percent. When this condition is reached, clouds will form, and the water vapor which is invisible will have become water droplets which the eye can see. On the ground this would be fog.

Keep in mind that air cools as it rises and warms as it descends. Therefore, when warm air containing a certain amount of moisture rises, it cools to the point of saturation, and a cloud is formed.

Western Montana mountains are responsible for many of our clouds, for as the air reaches these obstacles, it lifts, cools to saturation point, and becomes a cloud. As the air continues eastward and drops to the lower land it warms again and clouds decrease. Occasionally one will see a lone mountain which appears to be wearing a cap of clouds. To our eyes this cap appears stationary. However, it is forming on the windward side and evaporating on the lee side.

Another cloud phenomenon, often seen east of the Continental Divide, where the chinooks are active, is the lenticular cloud—in Latin an

Altocumulus cloud downwind of a mountain range. PHOTO BY TOM DIETRICH.

altocumulus lenticularis, or "middle cloud." They are most common during the fall and winter when westerly winds dominate, and may resemble lenses, flying saucers or pancakes, sometimes appearing stacked. When the sun is behind them they glow like pearls. Lenticulars form as the air, moving in waves over the mountains, reaches the crest of that wave. The cloud will remain in the same position even though the air is moving rapidly, and the principle characterizing its formation is the same as that of the cap cloud. Look for lenticulars late in the afternoon when a chinook is blowing and the sun is low.

The chinook winds bring us another outstanding cloud formation, the "Chinook Arch," found along the east slopes of the Rockies from Denver to Fort St. John in Canada. This is another manifestation of the lift of the air over the mountains causing a giant sustained wave of air with the clouds forming at the top of the wave. To an observer on the ground, it appears as a huge arch with a very smooth edge close to the mountains.It is an altostratus formation. The old-timers watched for signs of this cloud to tell when the chinook would arrive.

During the winter when wind conditions become stagnant and there is very little movement in the lower layers of air in the western Montana valleys, the low clouds will often form and remain packed tight against the mountains. This is especially true in the Flathead Lake area where the clouds will hide the eastern shore while the western shore is enjoying sunshine. The mountains act as a dam, holding the clouds and preventing them from moving on. The clouds are usually stratus during the night and change to stratocumulus during the afternoon.

Condensation nuclei are necessary for cloud formation. These are microscopic particles such as dust, smoke and salt crystals. The water vapor requires something upon which it can condense in order to produce clouds. Because of the abundance of these nuclei in the western valleys, clouds and fog are more prevalent than on the east side of the mountains where the air is more clean.

All of the state enjoys the spectacular beauty of the towering cumulonimbus which form in conjunction with the heating of a summer day. When the necessary amount of moisture is present and other conditions right, the heating that occurs will start air rising until it reaches that point at which condensation takes place, and the cloud begins to build. When the final stages of development have been reached, the top of the cloud will have reached the stratosphere. It then loses its rounded cauliflower form and becomes cirrus (ice crystals) in the shape of an anvil. A fully developed cumulonimbus is a complete small-scale weather system and can produce thunder, lightning, rain, snow, hail and extreme winds.

An interesting thing to note as one watches the clouds is the relative speed and direction at which they are moving. By using a pole, tree, or the corner of a building as a reference point, it is not difficult to determine this.

When there is more than one layer of clouds present, it may be seen that each layer has its own course depending upon the changing upper air movement.

•   •   •

Stratus, cirrus, cumulus, nimbus—science has handily categorized what we see drifting across our skies; but as for the romance of cloud-gazing? That's best left to the poets.

Umbrella Weather:
Types of Precipitation

by Grayson Cordell

All of us know what drizzle and rain are. Drizzle consists of small water droplets, larger than fog, that fall slowly to the ground, but may give the appearance of floating on air currents. Raindrops are larger. Usually the heavier the rain, the larger the raindrops. They may be nothing more than snowflakes that melted while falling through lower, warmer air layers.

Freezing rain occurs when warm air lies above a cold below-freezing layer of air on the ground. As the rain falls through the cold air, it becomes supercooled, freezing quickly upon striking the ground.

Sleet forms if the low layer of below-freezing air is thick enough for the raindrops to freeze before reaching the ground. Sleet is usually transparent pellets of ice that bounce upon hitting the ground.

Anyone living in Montana more than a few months knows what snowflakes look like. A snowflake is an ice crystal, or more commonly, an aggregation of crystals. Flakes as large as 10 inches in diameter have been reported falling from extremely calm air.

Snow pellets fall in brief showers in the cold season when the atmosphere is moderately unstable. They are white, opaque, round pellets of snowlike consistency and often burst when they hit hard surfaces. They are also sometimes called soft hail.

Hail is an interesting and spectacular form of precipitation. Hailstones range in size from ¼ inch up to more than 5 inches in diameter. They have an onionlike structure consisting of different layers of ice.

Hail almost always falls from a thunderstorm. The violent updrafts commonly associated with thunderstorms are necessary for the growth of the ice layers. Hailstones are formed by small ice pellets colliding with supercooled water drops. Part of the water freezes instantly, some remains attached to the growing hailstone until it freezes and probably some breaks away. The hailstone continues to grow rapidly as it strikes drop after drop of water during its fall, until it leaves that portion of the cloud containing supercooled water. It may fall into an updraft of air which carries it high into the cloud again, back into the same or another supercooled water region where the process is repeated.

This cycle can recur a number of times and will continue until the hailstones become too large for the updraft to support them or they fall free of an updraft zone. In falling they may encounter a new and even stronger updraft that sweeps them even higher into the cloud, perhaps tossing them out at the top where they fall to the ground through clear air. At other times, as the updraft weakens, the hail falls back through the cloud, growing bigger all the time.

Hailstorms are rare in the tropics and in the polar regions. They usually occur between latitudes 30 degrees and 60 degrees and are not common over oceans. Very strong vertical air currents are necessary, as well as freezing temperatures at relatively low altitudes. In the tropics, the altitude at which freezing temperatures are encountered is so high that the hail usually melts before reaching the ground. In the far north, updraft activity is too weak.

The areas of most hail do not correspond with the areas of heaviest thunderstorm activity. In the United States, thunderstorms occur most frequently in the southern states, but the most hailstorms occur over the western Great Plains and the Great Basin west of the Rockies. More than one thunderstorm in six is accompanied by hail in Cheyenne, Wyoming; but in Miami, Florida, only one in 71 produces hail.

RESEARCH

Lightning Lab at Missoula

by James E. Lotan & Donald M. Fuguay

The few fire researchers available during the '20s and '30s labored valiantly to understand fire behavior. Their studies, mainly conducted outdoors, made great progress, but eventually it became clear that new methods were needed. It was crucial to be able to control critical elements of the weather. New and exotic instruments as well as specially trained scientists became essential. A special laboratory was the answer.

The Northern Forest Fire Laboratory, a facility of the Intermountain Forest and Range Experiment Station, U.S. Forest Service, was dedicated on September 12, 1960. Located adjacent to Johnson-Bell Field near Missoula, the facility includes a 66-foot-high combustion chamber where fire researchers study scale-model fires under controlled air temperature, atmospheric pressure and relative humidity. In addition, high- and low-velocity wind tunnels enable researchers to study fire behavior in winds regulated up to 50 miles per hour. Early work involved basic studies to better understand fire hazard reduction, man-caused fires, lightning-caused fires, fire detection, fire behavior, fire suppression and how to use fire beneficially.

Early fire researchers had favored the direct approach. Consider Harry T. Gisborne's attempts at dissipating thunderheads by seeding them with dry ice. Gisborne persuaded Bob Johnson, the pioneer mountain pilot, to fly a C-47 into a cumulus cloud over Evaro Hill, a few miles north of Missoula. The airplane was designed to cruise at 10,000 feet and was not pressurized. Johnson was able to climb to about 25,000 feet. Some cold, logy, oxygen-starved researchers dropped one bag of dry ice over the side and landed again wondering what had transpired. In fact, they weren't even sure which cloud they had "conquered."

According to Gisborne, the "...widespread rain which began in Missoula about two hours after we scattered our ice, and the snow which stopped traffic on Evaro Hill that evening, occurred elsewhere throughout this section of Montana, and were the products of a general meteorological

Lightning blazes above Canyon Ferry Reservoir. PHOTO BY BOB HENKLE.

condition." But it was just as well that the motorists stuck on Evaro Hill did not know of the cloud-seeding attempt.

Subsequent trips were better prepared, but not without problems: inadequate communications within the plane, handwriting becoming worse in direct proportion to decreasing temperature, problems in dumping the ice out the open door of the C-47, and crude oxygen-breathing apparatus. Oxygen was sucked from a plastic tube. "That blast of oxygen coming out of a tube and directly into your mouth at 30 degrees below zero freezes [everything] from your adenoids to your tonsils, if you have any," Gisborne commented.

The problems with each man independently controlling his own oxygen supply led to some confusion, particularly when insufficient quantities caused a rapid decline in efficiency. One scientist would stand on the hoses of the others, or turn off the oxygen supply of his neighbor. Confusion mounted. As Gisborne stated, "I couldn't think and . . . didn't care if I didn't think!"

Fire researchers at the Northern Forest Fire Laboratory in Missoula have come a long way since Gisborne's early attempts to conquer thunderheads. Lightning and fire-weather meteorologists have developed methods of detecting and locating actual lightning strokes by remote sensing. A network of lightning detection locators can cover remote backcountry areas not easily observed by other means. We better understand the nature of fire weather and its role in fire behavior and predicting fire effects.

We have a fire behavior prediction system that predicts fire activity on a daily or other short-term basis. This system has been packaged for use in small, hand-held calculators that can be used in the field to predict fire intensity, rate of spread, and the probability that windborne embers will ignite new fires. A National Fire Danger Rating System measures and quantifies daily fire danger.

Fire suppression has been improved greatly. Chemical fire retardants and specialized aerial delivery systems have been developed and are routinely used by fire-control forces. Infrared scanners are used in aircraft to detect and photograph forest fires, even at night or through dense smoke cover.

A broader perspective of the natural role of fire has been developed, whereby we can better predict not only damaging effects of fire but beneficial uses. Prescibed burning guidelines have been developed for a wide variety of vegetative communities and fuel conditions. Scientists are now studying fire as an efficient management tool.

The complexity of fire research is illustrated by the disciplines studying fire at the Northern Forest Fire Laboratory. Research foresters, meteorologists, mathematicians, physicists, mechanical engineers, wildlife biologists, chemists, operational research analysts, ecologists and computer scientists combine talents to solve the complexities of Montana's weather and fire problems. Harry T. Gisborne might be amazed at the talents applied to problems that concerned him in 1949.

■■■■■■■■ANATOMY■■■■■■
OF A THUNDERSTORM

The summer thunderstorms that have such a profound impact on Montana's forests and grasslands are really quite mild compared to thunderstorms of the Great Plains, the eastern United States, and even some spring and fall storms in the Northern Rocky Mountains. But the storms occur during July and August when hot, dry weather has baked forest fuels. Also, the lightning is usually not accompanied with large amounts of rain and hail. Most storms do not exceed .05 inches of rain.

A typical thunderstorm begins as a small cumulus cloud that forms about noon and continues to build throughout the afternoon. The cloud attains great heights, resembling an anvil setting on a column. The base of the cloud will be at approximately 12,000 feet above mean sea level (m.s.l.), with a temperature of about 36 degrees. Temperatures within the cloud reach zero or below. The top of the cloud typically will reach about 36,000 feet to 40,000 feet m.s.l. Inside the cloud, water vapor condenses into large drops of water or ice. The particles fall through the center of the cloud, creating an accumulation of negative charges near the bottom of the thunderhead and positive charges at higher levels within the cloud. The negative part of the cloud attracts positive charges to the ground beneath it. Positive charges flow toward the thunderhead through hills, trees, rocks, buildings, people or whatever will conduct the charge. The charges build a voltage difference between cloud and earth of millions of volts. When the resistance of the intervening air is overcome—*zap*—we see a lightning bolt. A typical summer storm will produce about 100 electrical discharges, of which about 40 are cloud-to-ground flashes. The remaining strokes are between the charge centers within the cloud or into the surrounding air. Most of this activity takes place in a fraction of a

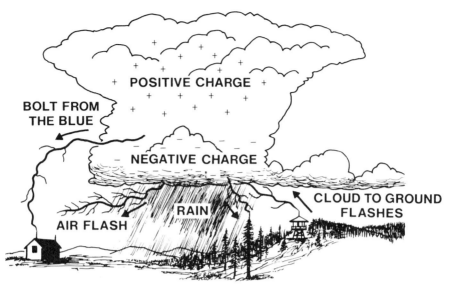

POSITIVE CHARGE

BOLT FROM
THE BLUE

NEGATIVE CHARGE

CLOUD TO GROUND
FLASHES

RAIN

AIR FLASH

Typical cloud-to-ground lightning. The small arrow indicates the direction of
the lightning leader.

second—a leader makes its descent from cloud to ground in a few thousandths of a second and a return stroke sends a surge of current up the channel in only a few millionths of a second.

Obviously, not all lightning bolts start forest fires. Research scientists have determined that fire-setting discharges are somewhat different than those that do not start fires. Ignition is most likely to occur when a lightning bolt has a long-continuing current during a return stroke. Temperatures may reach 50,000 degrees within the return stroke channel. In most cases, the fast strokes can have an explosive effect such as the splintering of trees, but it is the continuing current that ignites forest fires.

Although the summer thunderstorm over forested areas of Montana is quite modest in size and electrical activity compared to elsewhere, lightning bolts which strike snags, live trees, logging slash and accumulated forest debris produce a large number of forest fires each summer. Probably 70 to 80 percent of forest and rangeland fires are lightning caused.

Lightning plays many roles in Montana's biological communities. Some impacts are obvious; others are subtle and easily overlooked. Lightning discharges cause chemical changes in atmospheric nitrogen, which makes it available to plants. Lightning does not always kill a tree outright, it may weaken the tree, making it susceptible to insects and diseases.

Lightning striking a live conifer tree is a spectacular sight. The tree is often splintered and ruptured, as volatile oils, terpenes, finely divided bark, wood and needles are rapidly ignited. An intense ball of fire is created, which in turn ignites flash fuels in the tree crown or on the forest floor.

Wildfire can devastate forests and rangelands. Trees and shrubs are reduced to ashes. The landscape is blackened, the sky is filled with smoke. Soil is exposed to erosion. A beautiful forest is gone.

But there is another side to the role of fire in Montana's wildlands. The plant communities growing in Montana have remained essentially unchanged for 10,000 years or more—ever since the last major ice age. Our forest ecosystems exist not only in spite of these natural fire regimes, but also because of them. During this time, thousands of fires have been ignited naturally. These fires appear to have occurred on a cyclic basis, depending upon the kind of forest and location. Ponderosa pine forests near the floor of the Bitterroot Valley burned every six to 12 years; these were not stand-destroying fires, but surface fires. Other forests such as lodgepole pine and subalpine fir at high elevations probably did not burn except every 150 to 300 years. And many lightning ignitions never develop into large fires, but prevent fuel build-up and thus the much hotter, more damaging fires that would result.

Recurring fires have helped create a mosaic of vegetation. Some plants grow where fires are least likely to occur: moist areas, north-facing slopes and stream bottoms. Other species that survive repeated burning possess special features to cope with fire. Western larch trees have thick bark that insulates sensitive, inner tissues from heat damage. Ponderosa pine develop a thick, heat-reistant bark when exposed to fire. Many plants, particularly shrubs, resprout rapidly following fire. Many shrubs that are important big game food are rejuvenated by fire. Other plants such as lodgepole pine possess traits that enable abundant seeds to survive fire and thereby recolonize the site. Some lodgepole pine trees have special cones that do not open when seeds mature, but hold the seeds for many years until heat opens the cones. Thus millions of seeds per acre are released following a fire.

Fires also help prepare a seedbed where new plants can become established and grow—similar to rototilling a garden. Some plants require bare, mineral soil as a seedbed. Fire prepares the site.

Lightning occurring during the summer thunderstorm thus initiates change in Montana's forests and grasslands. Lightning fires in wilderness areas may be neither good nor bad, but simply part of a natural landscaping.The impact of fire in a forest ecosystem may not be fully apparent for decades and must be considered over the long term.

LIGHTNING PROTECTION

Some early foresters learned firsthand the nature of lightning strikes. On June 18, 1931, about 3 p.m. Murray Skillman and Richard Richtmyer left the top of Mt. Emerine on the Philipsburg Ranger District of the Deer Lodge National Forest. They were leading a pack string of eight horses. About a mile from the top as they rode under a telephone wire only 3½ feet above their heads, lightning struck.

When Skillman regained consciousness, he saw the entire pack string scattered about, tumbled in grotesque positions. Richtmyer lay on his side. His horse was getting up. Richtmyer tried to get up, but rolled over in pain. He had broken teeth and cuts about his face. It was several minutes before he regained his senses, but was able to later ride out. Skillman had a hole in his hat, hair burned above his ear, and a red streak along his collar bone and down his chest.

The lightning bolt had struck about a half mile above them and had burned the telephone line and wrecked the lookout tower on Mt. Emerine. Three men in a cabin at the foot of the tower were untouched.

Risk of death or injury from lightning should be of particular concern to outdoor people. There is little chance of being struck in a modern home or building. The city dweller is particularly safe, due to the sheltering effect of steel construction and grounded powerlines. Barns, haystacks and fences are especially vulnerable. Long rural telephone lines above ground are vulnerable. About 30 percent of lightning casualties are farmers or ranchers, but boaters, fishermen, swimmers, golfers, campers, picnickers are all susceptible. In short, any outdoor activities during summer months increase one's chances of danger.

Most lightning accidents occur in open areas. One fundamental rule is: Don't be a lightning rod! Do not become the tallest object nor stand near the tallest object unless it is an efficient lightning rod such as a tall tower or building. Such objects offer a zone of protection equal to one or two

A person can be injured not only by a *direct* strike by lightning, but also by *contact* with a conductor carrying the lightning current, a *side flash* from an object which has been struck, or by a *step voltage* from current passing along the ground from a nearby strike.

ZONE OF PROTECTION FROM A DIRECT STRIKE

A vertical lightning conductor such as a grounded radio tower, a building, or a power line, will give a zone of protection from a *direct* strike over a distance equal to 1 to 2 times its height. Note the unsafe zone within 3 feet of the conductor where a side flash can occur.

times their height. Stay at least two feet from a tower's legs to avoid side flash. Sitting in a car or truck with a metal top is excellent protection, but the metal top, not the rubber tires, protects you. An open tractor is particularly vulnerable because of its height in the field. The same is true of large animals. Do not stand near livestock or remain in the saddle. Four-legged animals are vulnerable to "step voltages"—that advance intermittently along the ground.

If you are caught on a high mountain ridge, and your hair begins to stand on end, or you feel a tingling in your fingertips, immediately crawl to a safer place. These signs are evidence that the lightning discharge process has begun.

And remember, it's the thunder that makes the noise, but it's the lightning that does the work!

Fire Weather: Montana's Mobile Fire Units
by Dave Goens

Sudden changes of wind direction or velocity may turn a routine blaze into a death trap. To meet the need for site-specific weather information, the Fire Weather Service was born in 1914 as a cooperative effort between the Weather Bureau and the U.S. Forest Service.

Interrupted by World War I, the project resumed in 1926. Eventually Missoula emerged as its center. The numerous fires that occurred in the Montana Rockies and the presence of the Forest Service Regional Headquarters were probably germane to Missoula's selection. In addition, weather records had been maintained there since the late 1800s. It was here that Ralph Hanna became the first official Fire Weather Forecaster.

Mobile weather unit, '50s-style. PHOTO COURTESY OF DAVE GOENS.

The *mobile* fire-weather station was developed in 1938, offering the flexibility to move observation to a wildfire and provide direct forecasts to the firefighters. The unit was simple, consisting of some weather intruments and a radio, a radio operator and a meteorologist.

In 1943, Wilbert R. Krumm, eventually known as "Mr. Fire Weather," replaced Hanna and expanded the program into a nationwide service.

By the 1950s firefighters were being accompanied by a panel truck turned weather station. The mobile units continued to evolve into the '60s when the Missoula Fire Weather District was split, placing eastern Montana under a Billings office.

Pickups with attached cab over camper units containing radio equipment allowed the forecaster to talk not only to his home station but to almost any base station in the West. Furthermore, he could make nearly independent forecasts if he lost his radio link with the home station.

Many infamous fires in the 1960s were supported by mobile weather units. The Sleeping Child Fire on the Bitterroot Forest, a product of lightning and strong winds, was ultimately controlled with the aid of such a unit. 1967 was a terrible year with nearly 1,500 lightning fires burning more than 75,000 acres. Mobile weather units from all over the West were detailed to western Montana and northern Idaho. Bob Thomas of the Billings office supported the Flathead Fire along the North Fork of the Flathead River during late August. A cold front moved through the area on August 23 and pushed the fire right through the fire camp! Thomas abandoned everything not attached to the truck and luckily escaped with little more than a terrible scare.

Other memorable fires supported in 1967 include the Sundance Fire in northern Idaho, Monture Fire near Ovando, and Canyon Creek Fire on the North Fork of the Flathead.

Most land-management agencies burn the residues from logging operations. Prior to and during a large burn, mobile units are called upon. During slash-burning season, 400 to 600 spot forecasts are requested annually. Mobile weather units also have been called during aerial application of insecticides over forested areas. Specialized site-specific forecasts are required to successfully spray rough mountainous terrain.

Such units have also assisted in the cleanup of Pacific Coast oil spills. Though none of the Montana units have been used, forecasters from Seattle and Los Angeles have taken part. They provide reports of winds, tides and ocean currents during the cleanup operations.

Montana's mobile units were updated again in the mid 1970s with the latest in solid-state radio equipment. Billings owns one, while Missoula has two units, one of which is owned jointly by the state of Montana and the Weather Service. This is the only such arrangement in the nation.

THE 1976 TOWNSEND SPRAY PROJECT

During late June and early July of 1976 the Fire Weather Service worked on the Helena National Forest during an aerial spray project to control spruce budworm in the Big Belt Mountains. The mobile unit was set up at the Townsend High School.

Spraying must be conducted at exactly the right time in bud worm development to be effective. Since development of the insects is controlled by temperature, weather is monitored at least one day in advance. The spray was to be applied as soon as it was light enough to fly each morning, for as soon as the temperature rose above 65 degrees the spray would no longer settle into the forest.

Before dawn each day the monitoring crew headed for the field. Occasionally the spray units were so far from Townsend, and the roads were so poor, that the monitoring crew spent the night on site. Equipment in the field monitored temperature and wind, and instrumented dirigible-shaped balloons equipped with sensors monitored temperatures as high as 300 feet above the ground. Spraying stopped whenever winds exceeded six m.p.h., for the insecticide would not settle.

While the meteorologist was in the field, the mobile weather station continued to produce the latest weather charts. As soon as the day's spraying was complete, the meteorologist returned to the unit to prepare the forecast for the next day's operation. These 16-hour days continued until the insects were too far developed to be effectively sprayed.

THE CABIN FIRE, AUGUST 1979

As equipment was updated in the 1970s, a new air-portable tent-trailer weather station was designed to be flown anywhere in the country on a transport aircraft, and then moved to the site of a wildfire via road or helicopter sling.

The fire season of 1979 was another bad one for the northern Rocky Mountains. Nearly 20,000 acres went up in smoke and nearly 12 million dollars were spent fighting the fires in Montana and northern Idaho. Southern Idaho sustained even higher losses.

The Fire Weather Mobile Units from Missoula and Billings were used from mid-July on, supporting the Deep Granite Fire which burned near Libby and the Barker Fire near Anaconda. I was assigned to the Barker Fire with the state mobile unit when the Cabin Fire broke out in the Scapegoat Wilderness Area north of Ovando. Since all regular Fire Weather Mobile Units were committed, an air-portable weather unit from Boise was brought in.

It was trailered north from Boise and I was replaced on the Barker Fire so that I could arrive in Missoula about the same time as the mobile unit. Before daylight the next morning we were on our way to the staging area along the North Fork of the Blackfoot on Kleinschmidt Flat, from which the unit would be airlifted into the fire camp.

Quite a crowd gathered as the Montana National Guard helicopter hovered over the little tent trailer unit. A sling was attached and the lift began slowly. I held my breath, the helicopter raised the unit about 20 feet off the ground, hovered for 30 seconds, and then lowered the unit. It was too heavy for them to lift safely unless stripped down and taken in two loads.

A fire was raging in the wilderness, this was to have been the first real test of the air-portable unit, and we could not get it into the air! The fire boss and his management team were screaming for a forecast. I had not seen a map or any data for six hours, but I jumped a helicopter and went in

Left: Caaaaaarefully. Helicopter drops weather forecast unit near Cabin Fire. **Right: Some cargo drops aren't this well organized. A load dropped too fast and high might mean a week's mop-up.**
PHOTOS BY DAVE GOENS.

to brief the fire team before catching the next helicopter out. We then dismantled the mobile unit.

Around noon the helicopter crew informed me that they would move the mobile unit in the evening when the temperatures cooled. With that assurance, and some new data I had picked up from a telephone conversation with the Missoula office, I hopped the next helicopter north and went back to the fire. I briefed the fire team again and with nothing else to do sat back and watched the fire burn up the canyon.

Just before suppertime, bad news arrived. Due to higher priority traffic the mobile unit could not be moved that day, but I was assured it would have top priority the next day. Meanwhile, I was a weatherman without his maps—frustrated indeed. At such times, you look at the sky, watch the smoke, stick your neck way out and make a good old fashioned guess. I didn't even have any cricket chirps to count or aching joints to inform me of pending rain.

It was a restless night on the mountainside. The crackle of a campfire can be soothing, but the roar of a forest fire and the knowledge that men are depending on a weather forecast you made by the seat of your pants is a little discomforting.

Shortly after sunup I heard the helicopter. As it neared I was overjoyed to see my portable weather station swinging gently underneath. It maneuvered into position, gently lowering its cargo on the site we had prepared. Considering the setbacks of the past day or so, I was not surprised to find the unit hung up on a stump when we went to move it by hand.

With the help of fellow forecaster Frank Gift from Boise we had the unit operational within an hour. Then the welcome voice of my boss Lloyd Heavner from the Missoula Office crackled over the radio. For the next hour, weather data came hot and fast. Charts were copied, weather reports and forecasts filed, and by midday I had prepared a forecast in which I felt confident. This was the way the operation was supposed to be handled! Unfortunately, it did not continue so smoothly.

By midafternoon Gift was on a helicopter back to the staging area. Southern Idaho was still burning and his services were needed. The Cabin Fire made a minor run that afternoon, and looked as if it would not be controlled for several days.

My mobile unit continued to work quite well the first two days. From my vantage point I could watch the west end of the fire and had an excellent opportunity to gather data for later research. Around mid-afternoon of the second day I was informed that there was to be an airdrop of supplies from an Air Force C-130 cargo aircraft. I was advised to be alert as the drop was to be targeted very near the mobile unit site. Having seen airdrops before, I temporarily abandoned the weather unit. The aircraft arrived about on schedule, but none of us were ready for what followed.

The terrain in the Scapegoat Wilderness is rough and when the air crew made its first pass for a look at the dropzone it's likely they had their hearts in their throats. All of the cargo had been rigged for a low level, slow speed drop, and the Air Force crew would not be able to get a C-130 down to treetop level at near-stall speed in that country. The next pass was to be a drop, and we all knew the craft was too high and too fast. Cargo began streaming out of the doors well before it should have and continued well after it should have. As the parachutes began popping open, about every third one tore loose due to the impact of the excessive drop speed. Supplies were strung for a mile up and down the canyon, and those bundles that had torn loose from their parachutes had exploded like mini-bombs when they struck the ground. As the aircraft passed over the mobile unit, one of the 'chuteless bundles looked as if it might go right through my hard-won forecasting equipment. I heard the bundle hit and thought it sounded serious. I was unable to check, for the air show continued more than an hour.

When the C-130 had completed its last pass I tentatively made my way back up the hill. Supplies were scattered over the mountainside and it would take more than two days to gather everything, a lot of it to be hauled out by packstring as junk and litter. As I climbed the last grade and saw my mobile unit, I breathed a sigh of relief. It was unscathed.

Hiplex: Miles City's Cloud-Seeding Experiment

by Bruce Bair

As long as there have been farmers on the High Plains, there have been rainmakers, who, for a fee, would unload their wagons of strange equipment, their bottles of hydrogen, their flash powders and proceed in full view of their sponsors to send their strange messages to the sky. Booming cannons were a favorite device since the Civil War, when it was noticed that torrential rains often followed battles. Hydrogen, often in balloons or sometimes flamed into the atmosphere, provided "levitating influences," huge charges of flash or gunpowder served the same purpose as cannons, and provided the added advantage of artificial lightning. Unbelievers were often convinced when rain came just as the methods were employed or soon after. One legendary Utah rainmaker was ridden out of town on a rail for his inability to stop the rain once he had started it. Often as not no rains came, and many of the makers, who wisely accepted payment only on delivery, moved on to the next town and tried again, where the weather might be more cooperative. Sensible pioneers did what the Indians did. They prayed for rain.

The rainmaking fraternity was shattered in the '40s by a chemist who had focused his attentions on cloud physics, while studying icing on aircraft. Irving Langmuir had won the 1932 Nobel Prize in chemistry, but it was the accidental discovery by his lab partner, Vincent Schaefer, which began the science of cloud seeding.

Both men were avid mountaineers and had observed during their climbs through cloud layers that clouds at high altitudes were composed of supercooled water droplets. Schaefer came up with a simple experiment. He breathed into a blackened, supercooled box, creating an artificial cloud of supercooled droplets—an experiment easily repeatable in the home deep-freeze. The scientists theorized that snow was formed when the droplets precipitated into ice crystals or snowflakes. They introduced dozens of finely ground substances into the cloud, trying to find a nuclei which would work.

Schaefer was unsuccessful until, on a warm day when the temperature in the box could not be kept cold enough, he introduced dry ice to cool the chamber. Immediately, the droplets changed to snowflakes and fell out of the artificial cloud. Through repetition of the experiment, Schaefer found that only the tiniest amount of dry ice was necessary to begin the chain reaction.

He was quick to see the implications of the experiment, and on Nov. 13, 1946, he seeded a cloud bank from an aircraft, and was delighted to see a large hole form in the cloud and snow falling below it. To make sure the initial success was not a fluke, the two men repeated the experiment, once even carving the emblem of their employer, General Electric, into a cloud.

Always flamboyant, Langmuir began predicting that weather would soon be controlled by man, and rushed off to experiments in New Mexico, where he claimed the production of billions of gallons of rain (and drew the ire of Texas farmers who claimed he was causing a drought) and in the Atlantic, where he seeded a hurricane, which promptly changed directions. In retrospect, Schaefer and Langmuir's experiments were far reaching, but premature. Their results could not be guaranteed against naturally occurring variations.

Another General Electric scientist, Bernard Vonnegut, using Schaefer's cloud chamber, discovered that silver iodide would cause the formation of ice crystals in clouds. To this day, dry ice and silver iodide remain the seeding mediums of weather modifiers.

Farmers were eager to seize upon the new technology, and by the mid-'50s were annually spending $5 million, often to send back-country pilots on seeding missions no more sophisticated than tossing chunks of dry ice into clouds from Piper Cubs. As much as 20 percent of the area of the U.S. was estimated to be affected by seeding. Interest waned in the '60s, with the annual turnover dropping to $2 million, and the area seeded to about five percent of the country.

A proponent of ground-based silver iodide generators, Irving Crick, was the first weather modifier to do business in Montana. Crick, who had made the weather predictions for the Allies on D-Day, was head of the meteorology department at Cal Tech when he became so interested in weather modification techniques that he quit his job and founded a firm of weather modification consultants. In the '50s, he set up a program near Miles City. At first, the experiments were paid for by the community, but later, the Tonn brothers, who ranch in the area, were so impressed by the technique they paid for half of the program.

"It really works," says Helder Tonn today. "It's more like milking the clouds than rainmaking, but a little extra rain can mean the difference between a good grass crop and a poor one." Though the Tonn brothers no longer have the generators on their range, they tied up any future supply of skyborne moisture. Theirs is the only ranch in Montana that has filed water rights on the clouds.

Other programs in and near Montana have been attempts to disperse fog at the Missoula airport with dry ice seeding. The state of Washington has carried on seeding operations to increase winter snowpack and summer rainfall. South Dakota had a statewide program which ended in controversy when some scientists claimed it did no good, and farmers blamed the program for creating drought. In Colorado, experimenters claimed a 20 percent increase in snowpack due to silver iodide seeding.

One weather maker whose appearances during dry years are reported regularly in Montana's rural press is F.N. Bosco and his Crop Improvement Institute. Claiming he is a student of Langmuir, Bosco explains at meetings of drought-weary farmers that his generators can "pull clouds from the sky." He promises rain within a week of setting up, inducing moisture, he says, with a handful of common chemicals, but he will not reveal what they are "since farmers would go out and buy them, and a slight excess might dry up the country."

Bosco has made periodic appearances since the mid-'70s, and has at times set up his equipment and claimed success, but he has never received a license to operate in Montana. His latest attempt was in 1980. Currently, the only holders of licenses in Montana are Crick, who was to have conducted seeding near Glasgow but was forstalled by fortuitous rains, and the state of North Dakota, which conducts operations along the border.

Montana became a center of national weather modification research in 1976, when Miles City was picked as one of the sites for the High Plains Experiment (Hiplex), an ambitious program to decide once and for all if seeding actually could increase rain on the High Plains.

According to Dr. Arlin Super, the site director, and his assistant from the beginning, Jack McPartland, the first task of Hiplex was simply to take a look at the naturally occurring clouds. "We didn't know enough to begin seeding," said Super.

Super is the picture of the dedicated scientist. Bearded, frequently wearing an immaculate lab coat, he can often be found looking into the screen of a computer, or in conference on the telephone with scientists in Boulder, Colorado, which is national headquarters for the whole Hiplex experiment. McPartland contrasts sharply. He is usually clad in cowboy boots, jeans and a plaid shirt, and enjoys week-long camping outings. But despite the contrast, the two have worked so closely together through the years that one often completes the thoughts of the other.

They experimented with silver iodide and various iodide generators, and then settled on dry ice as the seeding medium. "It worked better and there was no question of environmental danger," explained Super.

"We soon learned," he said, "that methods and measurements which worked in some parts of the world would not work in Montana, and that the rain-forming process was different here than in some other places. One of our earliest discoveries was that all precipitation in Eastern Montana begins with the formation of ice crystals."

Radar, it was found, was not adequate to measure the path of the rain. Without some idea of the actual 'product' on the ground, fashioning a statistically valid seeding experiment seemed impossible. A network of rain gauges, which were serviced weeky by young meteorologists on Honda all-terrain vehicles, was added to the design.

Problems continued and had to be solved. The small rain clouds on which Hiplex scientists planned to begin seeding experiments were often short-lived, and the research aircraft had difficulty reaching them before they dissipated. The solution was a Lear Jet seeding craft and a King Air, double turboprop observation craft.

A sleek Lear Jet was the Hiplex seeding plane. The average lifespan of the types of clouds being seeded is only 30 minutes, so the plane must be capable of reaching the cloud rapidly. PHOTO BY BRUCE BAIR.

The scientists intended to work with cumulus congestus clouds of specific sizes which are not copious rain producers. Often the rain they produce evaporates before it reaches the ground. The researchers felt they knew enough about this type of cloud by 1979, and intended to select 100 similar clouds and seed half. The unseeded clouds would serve as the control.

A few remaining bugs were worked out in the system during the early part of the '79 field season, but Mother Nature intervened. Though scientists expected 50 to 100 Hiplex-type clouds during the season, they were able to study only eight cases. Eastern Montana was in the midst of a drought.

A sophisticated network of automated weather stations was installed in anticipation of the 1980 season, but cowboys on the plains who arrived unexpectedly to observe the installation of the tripod supported instruments, or "spider joints," may have known more about what was going to happen during the summer of '80 than the meteorologists. "Does it measure dust?" one asked prophetically. The drought continued through 1980, and only 12 cases were studied. During the one week of summer that produced substantial moisture, the sophisticated ground network was down.

When the scientists analyzed their scant 20 cases, they determined that there was an 80 percent chance the seeding had produced additional rainfall. In fact, announced Super, rainfall in the seeded clouds appeared to have tripled, but he cautioned that no substantial additional quantities were reaching the ground, since the clouds were small producers anyway.

Seeding was scheduled to begin again in 1982. During the '81 season, the Hiplex staff joined with the National Center for Atmospheric Research and the Water and Power Resources Service of the Cooperative Convective Precipitation Experiment (CCOPE). CCOPE, the field portion of which was completed in August, was the largest and most comprehensive look ever attempted at plains thunderstorms.

A fleet of state-of-the-art business jets and turboprops bearing laser probes and suction samplers, a glider and an armor-plated military trainer for hail research were busy all season. Nature provided ample clouds, though spotty moisture, and the planes were airborne 75 percent of the days of the field season. Over 100 scientists and technicians participated, many housed in makeshift surplus mobile home barracks behind the hangars. They flew into everything from the small cumulus congestus clouds to monster thunderstorms. One aircraft was disabled for the season by softball sized hail. When the field season was over, Super was able to say that "good data sets were collected on every obective." Those included experiments on the role of electrification or lightning in storm development, learning more about the formation of hail, and with the aid of the greatly expanded network of automated ground weather station, determining the role of terrain and convergence on storm formation. The ultimate goals—better weather prediction and more precise seeding techniques.

Reagan's budget ax fell on Hiplex before the CCOPE observations began. Announcements were made that the program would not be continued, though funds are available to maintain a skeleton crew for data analysis through September, '82. Super says that analysis of the data obtained during the Hiplex and CCOPE experiments can answer, at least for small cumulus congestus clouds, the question, "does seeding make it rain?" He fears there will not be time to complete the work.

Staffers who have left, as well as Super and McPartland complain that it makes little sense to train staffs of meteorologists only to find funding cut off, leaving personnel to scurry toward other fields. They argue that in the future, funding is likely to be restored. The population of the world is still growing. More food will be needed.

"It could mean a lot of duplication," says Super. "By the time experimentation begins anew, these people will be in other fields. New experimentors aren't likely to use the old data. They'll collect their own data, when many of the questions could be answered right now. In the meantime, we're just scientists. We'll keep working on the data and hope for extended funding to keep working."

Wind Farm at Livingston
by Tom Livers

The wind is no stranger to Montana. For decades, mechanical windmills have pumped water at remote stock wells. Before rural electrification, the plains of eastern Montana were dotted with windmills bringing electricity to ranches and farmhouses. By the late 1970s, rising fuel prices brought about renewed interest in this almost-forgotten energy source.

Measured wind velocity has earned Livingston a ranking among the world's windiest cities. But miles-per-hour and foot-pounds can't capture the true character of the Montana wind as well as historian K. Ross Toole in the opening segment of his book The Uncommon Land:

"Does the wind blow this way here all the time?" asked the eastern visitor.

"No mister," replied the cowboy. "It'll maybe blow this way for a week or ten days, and then it'll change and blow like hell for a while."

• • •

The wind comes off the Pacific Ocean, 1,000 miles to the west. It sweeps across the plains of Washington, Oregon and southern Idaho before crashing into the towering peaks of the Continental Divide.

In the high country of Yellowstone Park, the wind is diverted down the Paradise Valley to Livingston, which receives the full force of the natural wind tunnel created by the Absaroka and Gallatin Ranges.

Old-timers say it's the only place on earth you can walk around the block and have the wind in your face every direction. They say if you're outside on a windy night and want to see what you're doing, you've got to have a friend hold the flashlight 10 yards upwind.

In quantitative terms this means an average annual wind speed of 16 m.p.h. Average speed in the winter is 21 m.p.h., with frequent gusts in the 80 to 90 m.p.h. range, all of which make Livingston a logical focus for Montana's wind-energy development efforts.

The state Department of Natural Resources and Conservation (DNRC) began intensive wind monitoring of the Livingston area in 1979. Data collected through this monitoring helped lay the groundwork for Montana's first non-residential wind generator, installed by the Montana Power Company (MPC) in May, 1980.

This generator represented a landmark in Montana's wind-energy development. With a rated capacity of 25 kilowatts (kw), it was the largest wind turbine in the state, and the first to be connected with the utility power grid. And it set the stage for further development of Livingston's wind resource.

Experimental in nature, the wind machine was not without problems. About a month after installation, a severe lightning storm caused a short circuit in the control system, despite the presence of a lightning rod above the turbine housing. The system continued to generate electicity in high winds, but when the wind died the turbine would actually draw power from the system and act as a huge motorized fan. The malfunction was discovered after about a week, and a lightning arrestor was installed to prevent further short circuits.

Despite the bugs, the system was successful. It worked well enough, in fact, that in the spring of 1981 DNRC's Renewable Energy Program awarded a $222,000 grant to Livingston to install four similar windmills to connect with the power grid and offset the energy needs of Livingston's new sewage treatment plant. In December, 1981, Livingston became the first city in the country to own a wind-powered utility when the four 25-kw turbines were installed.

Three weeks later, one of the four DNRC towers toppled, followed in a few hours by the MPC windmill a few miles away. The remaining three windmills were shut down and lowered.

For a while it appeared as if harnessing the Livingston wind would be harder than anticipated. An investigation by Multitech, Inc., the consulting engineer, and Jay Carter Enterprises, the manufacturer, proved that the extreme weather conditions of the Livingston wind corridor were at least partly to blame for the crash of the DNRC machine.

It started with a power outage. As a safety measure to prevent power surges during repair work, the turbines were designed to stop generating during an outage. This allowed the windmill propellors to free-spin, or rotate without turning the generator. As the propellor gained speed, a snubber mechanism was to change the pitch of the blades, causing them to slow and ultimately stop. Extremely cold temperatures, however, had thickened the hydraulic fluid in the snubber mechanism, causing it to malfunction. As a result, the propellor continued to gain speed until it threw a blade. The system's out-of-balance brake also malfunctioned due to cold temperatures, and the resulting stress on the tower caused it to topple. The exact cause of the MPC machine failure has not been determined, though a similar chain of events is suspected.

But it's hard to keep a good windmill down. By April, 1982, the four wind-farm towers were up, operating and awaiting their next challenge from the climatic forces they're attempting to harness. These weather extremes do provide a side benefit to wind energy development—the sustained high wind velocities coupled with the extremely low winter temperatures provide accelerated testing conditions for experimental wind turbines. The lessons learned at Livingston already have resulted in improvements to wind systems throughout the country.

THE BIG EVENTS

Mount St. Helens: Any Role in Our Weather?

by Grayson Cordell

On Sunday morning, May 18, 1980, Mount St. Helens in western Washington erupted, sending several hundred million tons of volcanic material into the atmosphere. The ash cloud above the volcano reached a height of 60,000 feet. The atmospheric shock wave reached Washington D.C. in a little more than three hours. From changes in air pressure there, the explosion was estimated to have had the energy equivalent of about 10 megatons of TNT.

Of the several hundred million tons of material blown into the atmosphere, probably less than a tenth were ash particles small enough to be carried long distances by winds. Even most of these would have had difficulty remaining aloft for more than a few days before returning to earth by fallout or being washed out by precipitation—the same processes by which the atmosphere cleanses itself of man's pollutants.

Of more concern were the estimated one million tons of very fine ash and some sulfurous gases that were lifted into the stratosphere at levels above 40,000 feet. At these altitudes the cleansing processes fail, as most weather systems do not reach these heights. There is extremely limited exchange of air with lower levels. These materials may remain aloft for months, or even years, dispersing into a thin veil of particles covering the northern hemisphere.

Fortunately, few gases of concern to us were produced by this eruption. The volcano was not hot enough to form nitrogen compounds. It also did not melt minerals, so little sulfur dioxide and few sulfates were present in the plume. Thus, St. Helens' veil was composed of mostly very tiny ash particles.

This veil intercepts a very small part of the incoming heat from the sun. Thus, a very slight cooling of the atmosphere could have resulted for a year or two, but its effect would have been inconsequential to us. Calculations show that any cooling that might have occurred would have been less than one tenth of a degree Celsius.

It also should be noted that volcanic eruptions occur every year, and any minor effect they may have is part of the earth's normal climate. The St. Helens eruption was only one of 10 eruptions that occurred worldwide in 1980.

Thus, most effects are of a local nature around Mount St. Helens due to the lack of vegetation and the barren thick ash cover, and some short term effects elsewhere that lasted only a few days under the ash cloud. This included Montana, especially the western portion of the state.

Near the volcano the air was highly charged with electricity, so highly charged that sparks jumped from the ice axes of climbers on Mt. Adams, 30 miles to the east. Eighty-five miles northeast of St. Helens, Yakima reported frequent thunder for more than six hours as the hot ash cloud drifted overhead. Snowfields near the volcano were melted and other snowpacks further away were covered with a thick ash cover that served as an insulation, greatly retarding snowmelt.

The main effect on Montana was the greatly reduced visibility from the ash fallout, the reduction of solar heating and decreased nighttime loss of the ground's heat while the plume was over the state. The thin ash deposit also changed the ground's reflectivity, slightly reducing the absorption of the sun's heat, but this effect was offset within a few weeks by vegetative growth.

It is unlikely the eruption contributed in any way to the drought that occurred in the Great Plains the next summer, the mild Montana winter that followed or any other weather events anywhere.

An eruption of St. Helens' magnitude is a rarity in this country, except in Alaska where several comparable eruptions occur each century. On a worldwide basis, eruptions of similar power occur ever two or three years. The most powerful eruption in modern times was that of Krakatoa in Indonesia in 1883. It is estimated that eruption was about 100 times more violent than St. Helens.

Of more legitimate concern is the April 4, 1982 eruption of Mexico's Chinchonal volcano. It blew at least 10 times more material into the upper atmosphere than Mt. St. Helens. Undoubtedly many weather phenomena will be attributed to this eruption, but it will be years before we can determine any real effects.

PHOTOS COURTESY OF NATIONAL WEATHER SERVICE

Rather dramatic pictures were taken of the Mount St. Helens eruption at 9:46 a.m. on May 18, 1980. (Picture A) The rapid eastward movement of the dust cloud was very evident on the ensuing pictures. The first picture of the initial eruption was available to National Weather Service weathermen within minutes after the occurrence. Picture B was taken by the polar orbiting satellite, which is at a considerably lower altitude than pictures A and C, which were taken by a geo-stationary satellite. Picture B also shows how the dense ash cloud flattened out on top as it bumped into the warm inversion layer beneath the stratosphere. The westerly winds aloft then started carrying the suspended dust eastward. Picture C shows the volcanic dust cloud spreading into western Montana 10 or 11 hours after the eruption. (William Rammer)

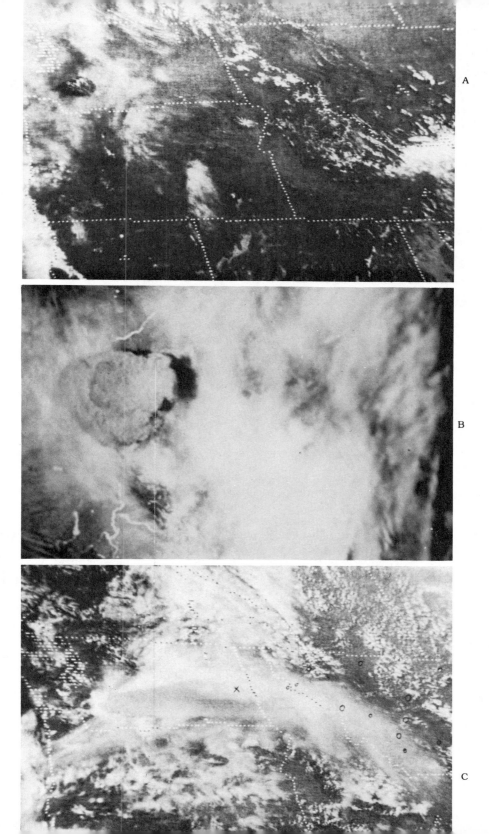

A

B

C

Winter of Calamity 1886-'87

by George D. Mueller

Montana has experienced a number of hard winters throughout its history, but none has equalled the winter of 1886-1887 in human misery and loss of livestock.

It was during this winter that Charles Russell was working for the O-H Ranch near Utica. When the ranch foreman had to advise the owners in Helena that their herd had perished in this terrible winter, Russell pulled his watercolors out of an old sock and sketched his 2x4 masterpiece of a starving cow humped over in the snow, about ready to keel over, while hungry coyotes waited patiently for their meal. The sketch entitled "Waiting for a Chinook" is more popularly known as "Last of the Five Thousand" and is perhaps the most famous of all his works.

The spring of 1886 found the cattle in eastern Montana in fine condition with the calf crop unusually large. Indeed, one large operator, Granville Stuart of the DHS Ranch, reported branding about 3,900 calves in the spring of 1886 from 18,900 cattle the previous fall. The Stuart home ranch was in Central Montana on Ford Creek, about three miles from the foot of the Judith Mountains and adjoining Fort Maginnis. The spring roundup had been exceptionally large. For example, the Judith Roundup at Utica amounted to an estimated 25,000 head, represented principally by the True, Hobson, Schaffer, and Kaufman-Stadler outfits. The Flat-willow pool was said to run as high as 56,800 and there were numerous smaller roundups about the country.

As may be surmised, the range was overstocked. Added to the problems of overstocking, the spring of 1886 had been very dry and the grass was poor.

As early as May, conditions were becoming serious. Official Signal Corps records from Fort Custer, at the confluence of the Big Horn and Little Big Horn Rivers near present-day Hardin, show that May was extremely dry with only a little over one-half inch of moisture and with many days over 90 degrees and several near 100 degrees. Farther north at Fort Assinniboine a few miles southwest of present-day Havre, similar conditions were reported.

Normally, June is Montana's wettest month, with moderate temperatures. Such was certainly not the case in 1886. The maximum temperature at Fort Assinniboine seldom went below 80 degrees after the middle of June, and during the last week was below 90 degrees only one day, reaching as high as 95 degrees. Only a little more than three-fourths of an inch of rain was recorded.

July started out hot, still, and extremely dry. Temperatures of 90 degrees to 95 degrees were common with little or no rain. On July 8, 1886, Pvt. Charles Trotter of the Signal Corps at Fort Assinniboine reported the following: "Maximum temperature, 104 degrees, the highest recorded since this station opened. Mean temperature for the day, 77.8 degrees. The water supply at this post is almost exhausted. Stock on the ranges are suffering from want of water. The prairies present the appearance of having been burned by fire." A few days later, the temperature hit a blistering 108 degrees. At Fort Custer, the maximum temperature remained below 90 degrees on only eight days during July and there were many days over 100 degrees.

Despite severe drought, cattle were being brought in from Washington and Oregon, in addition to the large herds from the south, and were thrown into the already overstocked ranges of Montana. By the fall of 1886, there were more than one million head of cattle on the Montana ranges.

By August, the ranges of eastern Montana were critically dry. Creeks and water holes, never before dry, were bone-dry. The combination of many days of 100-110 degree weather with hot dry winds began to take its toll in prairie fires. From Aug. 9, 1886, the Signal Corps weather observer at Fort Assinniboine reported numerous prairie fires in the vicinity; and on Aug. 26, the log indicated .10 inches of rain extinguished a prairie fire which burned 300-400 square miles, destroying the best grazing north of the Missouri River and timber in the Bear Paw and Little Rocky Mountains.

Farther south at Fort Custer, Sgt. Edward Beals, Signal Corps Weather Observer, reported 105 degrees on two consecutive days in August and the following, "Weather almost suffocating. All vegetation burned and dry as if it had been in a fire."

A forewarning of things to come appeared in the Great Falls Tribune of Sept. 11, 1886. It reported only about two inches of moisture in the last year. The writer further states, "Much depends upon the coming winter. If it is one favorable to flocks and herds, there need be no thought taken of this remarkable year, other than as a matter of curious meteorological history."

With the approach of autumn, some of the old-timers were predicting an open winter. In a report from the Great Falls Tribune of Oct. 23, 1886, one prominent cattleman of Fort Benton stated, "It has always been my experience that when we had a dry summer, an open winter followed."

Autumn, however, did have every appearance of a severe winter. Old timers noted fewer beavers left in the country and they had piled up abnormal quantities of saplings for winter food. Granville Stuart, in his book "Forty Years on the Frontier" reported, "This year, we noticed that the wild animals moved south. The wild geese, ducks and song birds started south early and many that were accustomed to stay with us all winter, disappeared. Even the range cattle seemed to take on a heavier, shaggier coat of hair. For the first time since I had come to the range, the white Artic owls came on the range and into the Judith Basin. The old Indians pointed to them, gave a shrug, and said 'Ugh! Heap cold!' "

"One old Gros Ventre assured me that not since he was a small boy had he seen the owls on their reservation."

Winter started with an arctic outbreak that covered the whole country from the Rocky Mountains to the eastern states. Central Montana was, as usual, hit the hardest. There were 6 inches of snow on the level and, combined with strong northerly winds, it blew into drifts. The Great Falls Tribune of Nov. 27, 1886, reported the late blizzard had caused heavy losses of sheep and a large herd had drifted into the Teton River and the herder had frozen to death. This storm was followed by a couple days of drizzling rain that turned the snow to slush. The wet snow froze into a hard crust and cattle were unable to feed. The temperature then plunged below zero.

There was some let-up in mid-December followed by a storm beginning on Christmas Eve. It was accompanied by high winds and the temperature fell steadily. By Christmas night, the temperature at Fort Assiniboine had dropped to -22 degrees and to -37 the next day. The Missouri River at Fort Benton was frozen solid by Dec. 27 and teams were crossing on the ice.

January, 1887 started off with a very severe storm on New Year's Day. The Great Falls Tribune of Jan. 8, 1887, reported the heaviest snowfall since 1881 and the depth on the level at Fort Maginnis was 16 inches.

Farther north at Fort Benton, a fuel famine was beginning to be felt. The River Press of Jan. 5, 1887, reported, "Coal is in urgent demand." The shortage of coal was largely due to the severe drought of 1886; and due to low water, the steamboats could not get to Fort Benton and had to off-load at points farther down the river. Teams could not get through the deep snow to bring in fuel.

Excerpts of a letter written by David Hilger to Andrew Fergus on Jan. 9, 1887, from Christina, Montana, describes the mood of the ranchers. "I have lately been thinking of the man that composed. 'O the snow, the beautiful snow. Filling the sky and the earth below.' and I have come to the conclusion that he was neither a cowboy nor a sheepherder; suppose we transpose it a little and read thus;

"O the snow, the abundant
snow
Filling the sky and the earth
below
Causing sheep to 'hump' and
cattle to moan

Covering the last morsel that is in sight until the last thought has actually flown of ever seeing spring so friend 'good night.' "

A report from Fort Keough dated Jan. 8, 1887, reported, "The weather last night was the coldest of the season. The spirit thermometer at the post hospital registered 50 below zero, which is their minimum, but it must have been much colder." By the middle of January, the snow was so deep that stagecoach drivers were having a hard time and had to follow the telegraph poles on their routes.

The post paper at Fort Keough reported a temperature of -60 on Jan. 14, 1887, and the snow was two feet deep.

A week later, the River Press at Fort Benton reported snow two feet deep on the level and only about 100 sacks of flour left in town. Coal oil was scarce and was selling at $6 per case.

Faced with continuous strong northerly winds and severe cold, the cattle began to drift southward. They were unable to cut through the heavy crust to feed. Their noses were cut by snow granules and became raw, bloody and swollen. Some broke through the crust and lacerated their legs. Others stood until their lower extremities were frozen and finally lay down never to rise again. Many cattle drifted into coulees and along river banks.

By the third week in January, the fuel situation in Fort Benton was becoming desperate. About half the town had enough fuel to last 30 days. Snowfall at Fort Benton had been 32 inches from Dec. 1 to Jan. 20.

As the end of January approached, the livestock situation had become grave. The River Press at Fort Benton of Jan. 26, 1887, reported, "There are grave fears of severe loss of livestock on adjacent ranges. Everyone tries to make a cheerful view of the situation, but a general feeling of uneasiness cannot be suppressed."

Snow was nearly two feet deep and crusted in most places. It was six to eight feet deep in nearby Yellowstone Park. A Northern Pacific special with three engines bucked snow for six days between Livingston and the Park.

The worst storm of the season was raging on Jan. 29. At Fort Maginnis, it was snowing hard and the wind was blowing 60 mph with the mercury at 14 below zero. Cattle were suffering dreadfully and many perished. It was no wonder, as this combination of wind and temperature gives an equivalent temperature of better than -80 degrees. This "great storm" lasted through Feb. 4, 1887.

By Feb. 1, the temperatures were the lowest of the winter. At Fort Assiniboine, the temperature dropped to -47 degrees on the first, -48 on the second, and a record breaking -55 on the third. The official Signal Corps report of Feb. 3, 1887, read, "Minimum temperature last night, -55.4; the lowest ever recorded. Extremely high and almost stationary barometer. Mean corrected barometer for the day, 39.9, the highest on record at this station. Owing to the deep snow on the ground and the long continued cold weather, many cattle throughout this section are dying, coaches are delayed two and three days and travel is entirely suspended." There were, also, brisk winds inducing an equivalent temperature of around -95.

Further east, E.C. "Teddy Blue" Abbot was riding for Granville Stuart on the DHS range. He reported the worst blizzard he had ever seen on Feb.

3 and 4. The cattle drifted down on the Missouri and Milk Rivers and thousands went through the air holes in the ice. Their horses' feet were cut and bleeding from the heavy crust and cattle had the hair and hide worn off their legs to the knees and hocks. The cowpunchers worked hard to get the cattle back in the hills in a blinding snowstorm with temperatures 50 to 60 below.

Conditions in Fort Benton went from bad to worse. The Great Falls Tribune of Feb. 5, 1887, reported that only the wealthy could afford coal oil. Flour and sugar were running short. Coal was selling at $30 per ton, cash. There was much thievery. The River Press of Feb. 9, 1887, reported that the old jail was torn down and used for firewood. An offer of $60 per ton for coal was refused by one owner. Fences were being cut down for fuel. Families were clubbing together and occupying the larger houses to save fuel.

Still another blizzard hit on Feb. 15. The River Press of Feb. 16 reported that the average temperature at Fort Assinniboine for the first ten days of February was 20 degrees below zero.

By the middle of February, Fort Benton was nearly out of both fuel and food. The following prices were quoted from the Great Falls Tribune of Feb. 19, 1887, "Flour, $7 per sack; coal, $50-60 per ton; green willow wood, $20 per cord; potatoes, not to be had at any price." The thermometer froze at -50 at Fort Benton on Feb. 15.

There was still no break in the weather. The River Press of Feb. 23, 1887, reported it took two days to go from Great Falls to Fort Benton. Parties returning from the Bull Mountains reported many dead cattle. Many were buried in the snow standing up with only their horns visible. There were many conflicting reports of losses. Some were too optimistic. The losses of sheep in Meagher and Fergus Counties were figured at least 10,000 head. However, the fuel situation had eased in Fort Benton.

Finally, the long awaited chinook arrived and the temperature at Fort Assinniboine reached 46 degrees on Feb. 27 and 28. The snow disappeared almost overnight and the sudden thaw caused a disastrous flood on the Missouri River, doing great damage at Bismarck, N.D.

The plains, streams, and coulees of eastern Montana were not a pretty sight. Cattle and sheep carcasses were to be seen almost everywhere. There were many conflicting figures on losses and it was difficult to arrive at accurate figures. The Great Falls Tribune of March 5, 1887, reported at least 200 head of dead cattle on the Missouri River between Giant Springs and Rainbow Falls, a distance of only about two miles.

The heaviest losses were among the "pilgrims" brought in from the east, milk cows, calves, and bulls. "Teddy Blue" Abbott in his book, We Pointed Them North, said the loss on trail cattle that had just come into the country was 90 percent. He stated that fully 60 percent of all the cattle in Montana were dead by March 15, 1887. Double-wintered Texas steers in the Big Dry country got through the best shape of any cattle in the state.

The large outfits were hit the hardest. Most had borrowed large sums of money at a high rate of interest and were deeply in debt. Many had to start all over again. Granville Stuart probably best summed up the feelings of many of the cattle barons by stating, "A business that had been fascinating to me before, suddenly became distasteful. I wanted no more of it. I never wanted to own again, an animal that I could not feed and shelter." Some of his cattle were still being gathered up in July on the Maginnis range. They were weakened and "gaunted." One old fellow working with "Teddy Blue" Abbott, the sweat pouring off his face, looked up at the sun, and sober as a judge said, "Where the hell was you last January?"

The surviving cattlemen had learned their lesson well. This was the end of the open-range cattle business. No longer were cattle left out in the elements to fend for themselves without feed or water, and it was the beginning of modern feeding methods.

The Weather and the Infantry at Fort Shaw

by Dick Thoroughman

*Women and babes shrieking awoke
To perish 'mid the battle smoke
Murdered, or turned out there to die
Beneath the stern, gray, wintry sky.*

These words were written in 1870 by a 19th century humanitarian who used them as part of a condemning testimony against the actions of the United States Army in Montana Territory. The harsh lines referred to an incident that involved three primary ingredients in the history of the West: the United States Army, the Indian and the weather. On the morning of January 23, 1870, a combined force of the 2nd United States Cavalry from Fort Ellis, Montana Territory, and the 13th United States Infantry from Fort Shaw, Montana Territory, commanded by the Major Eugene M. Baker, struck a Piegan village on the banks of the Marias River in north central Montana. It was a one-sided engagement fought in intolerable cold, and it was to provoke an outcry from eastern humanitarians. Though the Army tried to defend its actions, it was condemned in the eastern newspapers. In the eye of the public, the United States Army stood convicted of " an unspeakable act of barbarism."

Fort Shaw, which played a large part in this notorious battle, was located on the banks of the Sun River some five miles west of the community of Sun River Crossing, where the Mullan Road crossed the Sun. In considering the weather and its role in Montana history, the Sun River Valley is unique, for records from this region are very old in comparison to other areas of our state. In fact, the earliest written weather record appears in 1805, penned by Captain Meriweather Lewis.

Again, much later, in May 1875, the U.S. Surgeon-General's Report, prepared for the War Department, examined the weather conditions found at Fort Shaw. ". . . the valley is almost destitute of water, aside from the river." The report further stated that the climate was "exceedingly dry all the year round," and that "snow rarely lies on the ground long after a storm. High westerly winds prevail and drive much of the snow into drifts;

at the same time the current of dry atmosphere moving over the surface melts the snow, and bears away the moisture quite as fast as melted. The diurnal oscillations of temperature, however, are usually quite marked at all seasons of the year."

Someone, probably connected with the medical staff at Fort Shaw, made three daily observations and recordings of the temperatures at 7 a.m., 2 p.m., and 9 p.m., and the reports always made note of the extreme temperature variation found in the summer months. The report also stated that "The heat of the summer is quite inconstant; a high temperature rarely obtains for more than three of four days in succession. In the winter, likewise, the periods of intense cold are infrequent, and scarcely continue for more than a week at a time . . . winds are exceedingly prevelant at all seasons of the year, though they relax somewhat during the summer months. The location of the post is very favorable to catch the full force of the winds." In regard to the wind speed the report stated that the monthly average on a day-to-day basis was some 20 miles per hour. The following is the meteorological report for Fort Shaw, covering July 1870 through June 1871.

MONTH	TEMPERATURE		
	Mean	Max.	Min.
July	72.87	101	54
August	61.54	102	24
September	56.42	94	22
October	45.56	88	6
November	40.85	62	8
December	25.65	54	-13
January	25.48	60	-20
February	26.92	56	-28
March	35.53	54	14
April	41.69	72	26
May	56.57	78	37
June	70.63	92	48

As we can see, the highest recorded temperature at Fort Shaw in this time span was 102 degrees in August; and 28 degrees below zero, the coldest point, occurred in February. Note that it froze in August, with a 24 degree reading!

Also of interest are the earliest weather readings from Fort Shaw, from the year 1868, and they must be some of the oldest continuous weather records in Montana. In that year, the Geographical Department of the Army made a survey of the posts along the frontier and compiled a weather summary in which they noted the monthly averages for each post,

FORT SHAW, MONTANA TERRITORY 1868

Month	Average Temperature
January	11°
February	30°
March	40°
April	47°
May	52°
June	64°
July	71°
August	68°
September	50°
October	47°
November	36°
December	26°

The 13th Infantry had a most difficult time with the weather while they were stationed at Fort Shaw, during the years 1867 through 1870. Most had been transferred from the eastern theatre following the Civil War; thus, for the most part, Montana Territory's sudden blizzards and rapid chinooks were alien to them.

When the men were granted a pass, they broke the monotony of army life by heading into Sun River Crossing. On the night of November 28, 1867, a number of soldiers were in Sun River Crossing on a 24-hour pass, and since they were infantry, they had simply walked down or perhaps had caught rides with passing freight wagons. One of the soldiers who happened to be in Sun River Crossing that night was 18-year-old Private Daniel H. Lee. Private Lee had been seen in a number of drinking establishments that night and appeared to have become very intoxicated before he disappeared. His disappearance was not alarming to anyone since it was thought that perhaps he had gone to a hotel, or perhaps was with a prostitute, or had crawled into a pile of hay in one of the stables. When the rest of the men started back for the fort the following morning, they discovered his body lying beside the road at the outskirts of the settlement. He had been very intoxicated and had apparently decided to head back to the fort. After travelling a short distance, he had simply sat down and frozen to death—the first casualty of Fort Shaw.

• • •

Since Fort Shaw was the regimental headquarters, it had a large garrison of troops and this made it necessary to keep a large supply of stores on hand at all times, enough to sustain the post for a period of 10 to 12 months. "Stores" were such consumable items as food, medical supplies, clothing, ammunition and powder, hardware, etc. Since Fort Benton was the head of navigation on the Missouri, it was also the supply point for Fort Shaw, and it was the practice of the Army to re-supply the garrison three or four times a year. Steamboats would arrive at Fort Benton with supplies, and the Army would then contract with freighters to transport the stores overland via the Mullan Road to Fort Shaw, and because of the size and nature of the shipments, a large escort was always involved. Usually, two or three companies would march from Fort Shaw to Fort Benton and then escort the supply train back to Fort Shaw, at which point some wagons might go on to Helena. Others would be provided a safe return to Fort Benton.

Army records from Fort Shaw indicate that the winter months of January, February and March, 1869 had been unusually warm and supplies were reaching Fort Benton by mid-to-late March, for much of the ice was off the Missouri. On March 15th, Colonel I.V.D. Reeves, Commander, 13th U.S. Infantry, Fort Shaw, Montana Territory, sent three companies, B, D and H, to Fort Benton under the command of Major W.W. Prentiss. The command arrived in Fort Benton on the afternoon of the 18th after which preparations were made for their return to Fort Shaw on the 22nd. Again, the weather was noted as being unusually warm for this time of the year, and it made for a leisurely and almost enjoyable pace.

On the afternoon of the 24th, the command was a few miles to the northeast of The Leavings (present location of Vaughn) and some 34 men from H Company had been assigned to act as the rear guard for the supply train. The rear guard followed about one mile behind the main column, always maintaining visual contact with the supply train. When the blizzard struck, it was estimated that the rear guard contingent was slightly more than a mile behind the supply train. Because of the warm weather, reported as being near 60 degrees, the men had taken off their heavy winter clothing, coats, gloves, hats, etc., to be carried on ahead by the supply train. Remember, most of these men had been stationed in Montana Territory only a short time and had never experienced such an assault by the weather.

In the investigation held at Fort Shaw, all testimony indicated that the storm had been upon them in an instant. Some men said that in looking across the prairie to the north, they had seen the cloud bank, but were unable to judge its distance from them, and that the wind suddenly roared like thunder and then they were literally engulfed in the white swirling mass.

The supply column was about four miles north of present Manchester when they were swept up in the storm, the wind driving the heavy wet snow into their faces. Some of the teamsters said that as the blizzard struck, their mules reared and tried to escape their harness, and one outrider was actually thrown from his horse, which then galloped off into the blizzard, to be found a few days later in the brush along the Sun River.

The men in the main column scrambled for their coats and winter clothing as the teamsters turned their teams so that the rear of the wagons faced the storm and then they got off and took shelter with the soldiers under the wagons.

Prentiss realized what was happening to the rear guard, and his first thought was to send a rescue party with winter clothing, but with great reluctance he withdrew rescue orders, for visibility was gone.

The blizzard struck at approximately 3:30 p.m., and it did not abate for nearly an hour and a half, by which time the temperature had plunged

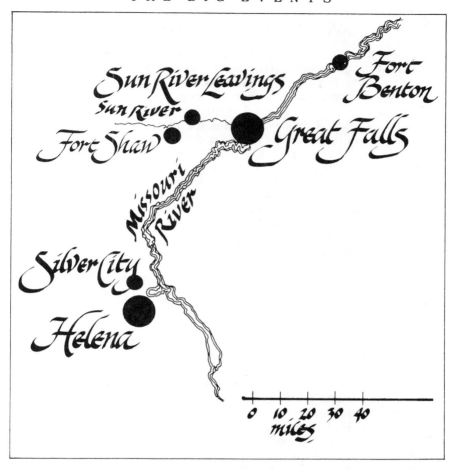

nearly 50 degrees. When the storm had first hit, the heavy, wet snow clung to everything and formed a virtual sheet of ice, but as the temperature dropped, the snow took on a much finer, almost sand-like quality. Driven by the strong winds, it cut into any face turned toward it. At about 5 p.m. the storm subsided as quickly as it had arrived, and clearing skies added to the chilling temperatures.

No time was wasted in organizing a rescue party. Using lanterns from the supply wagons, they set out to locate the rear guard and ultimately search for survivors. Because of the deep snow and gathering darkness, they had difficulty in determining the men's location. It took nearly an hour to reach the first man and establish the search area. Within the next hour, some 20 men had been found and taken back to makeshift shelter at the wagons. The bodies of nine men were found. In some cases it was difficult to determine the cause of death, for while it was obvious that some had frozen, others had fallen into small depressions in the ground, and were covered by the snow to such an extent that they may have suffocated. Despite the fact that the search continued all night, the bodies of five men remained unaccounted. Survivors were in serious condition. To alleviate some of their suffering, fires were started using whatever would burn from the wagons.

At first light, the column struggled out toward The Leavings, but because of the deep snow, nearly eight hours were consumed in travelling these few miles. It was shortly after noon on the 25th that they reached The Leavings, having fought for every step. The men and animals were exhausted and Prentiss ordered them into camp, utilizing barns, outbuildings and any place that they might find shelter and some warmth. Two more men had died during the night and a third died shortly after their arrival at The Leavings. The final death toll was 17. After a brief rest and some food, Prentiss sent riders ahead to Fort Shaw and Sun River Crossing to summon doctors and alert the post hospital to prepare to treat the men for frostbite. Reeves sent two mounted companies to The Leavings immediately; they arrived there during the evening of the 25th, bringing two doctors with them. The following day, they fashioned wagon bodies into sleds and transported the injured men up the valley to Fort Shaw. One company returned to the site of the disaster and recovered the remaining bodies.

In the days that followed, an investigation was held and it was ruled that no one had been negligent in any manner and no charges were leveled. It was ruled an Act of God.

• • •

The weather was to play another prominent role in the career of Fort Shaw, during the "Baker massacre" of January 23, 1870.

During the summer of 1868 and 1869, the Piegan Indians had relatively free rein in Montana Territory, and this put great pressure on the Army to take some kind of action against them. Fort Ellis, established August 27, 1867 near present Bozeman, was the only other post in the Territory. Upon these two commands fell the demand for action.

The orders and directives for this expedition were relayed through the ranking officer for the Territory, Philippe Regis de Trobriand, commander at Fort Shaw, to mount a campaign and expedition against the Piegans. A strongly worded message was wired to de Trobriand to launch his campaign and to strike the Indians and strike them hard.

Four companies of the 2nd United States Cavalry journeyed from Fort Ellis to Fort Shaw in January of 1870, in severe winter conditions. By the time they left Fort Shaw, they had been reinforced by a mounted company of the 13th Infantry, as well as a detachment of 13 men designated as sharpshooters.

After final preparations, the column departed Fort Shaw at approximately 10 a.m. on January 19, 1870. It has been noted that although the regimental band managed an appearance to hail their departure, the temperature hovered near 30 below. Despite the fact that the men were dressed in heavy winter clothing, it soon became apparent that they could not stay mounted for long without hampered circulation. They dismounted frequently in an attempt to stay warm.

Despite this added hardship, the column made good progress during the day, covering nearly 20 miles before they pitched camp close to Priest

Butte, near today's Choteau. The command remained in camp throughout the following day, for Major Eugene M. Baker, 2nd United States
Cavalry, was taking precautions against detection by avoiding a daylight
march.

The march resumed, reaching its objective on the bitter cold morning of
the 23rd. By 8 a.m., Baker's men were deployed around the surrounding
bluffs which covered a Piegan village on the banks of the Marias River. It
as a one-sided engagement fought in temperatures close to 35 below zero.
When it was over, the Indian village had some 173 casualties, plus
numerous prisoners. Approximately 300 of their horses also were cap-
tured. This was the battle that sparked such public outrage. The weather
had figured greatly in its inhumane outcome.

Flood Years
by John W. Fassler

Flooding occurs almost annually somewhere in Montana. Much of the
flooding is confined to river-bottom land used for agriculture. Most Montana floods have occurred in May and June when seasonal large-scale
meteorological conditions have been similar. Heavy rainstorms along and
near the eastern side of the Continental Divide in late May and early June
are clearly associated with floods of 1927, 1938, 1948, 1953, 1964, 1975
and 1981. However, it was the intensity of the June 7 and 8, 1964
rainstorm that makes the flood of that year the most devastating and spectacular on record in Montana.

All ingredients necessary for heavy rain in the affected area were present: (1) a large supply of relatively warm moist air (2) lifting of this air by
several methods, (3) large scale atmospheric motions that sustained these
overlapping effects for several hours.

Early in June, moist air from the Gulf of Mexico was spreading north-
northwest over the western plains and central Rocky Mountains. By the
afternoon of June 7th, when rains associated with the flood started, the air
mass carrying much of its original Gulf of Mexico moisture was entering
the northeast quadrant of a low-pressure area centered over Wyoming.

A strong flow from an easterly direction over north-central Montana was
travelling upslope in the heavy rain area—sharply upslope the last 10
miles or so just east of the Rocky Mountain ridge. It was during this period
of strongest upslope flow that rainfall rates were 0.50-1.00 inch per hour,
resulting in total rainfall values of 14 to 16 inches in some areas, and 10 to
12 inches in an area parallel to the Continental Divide from Rogers Pass to
Waterton Lake, Alberta, Canada.

A cold front entered the northern area of heaviest rains early on the
morning of June 8th. As this front moved slowly south, it continued to
supply winds from the northeast and vertical lifting of the air mass, thus
extending the duration of heavy rain by about four hours. Water stored in
the mountain snow pack was below average on the 1st of March in 1964,
but that reversed itself the next two months. By May 1 the stored water

Great Falls during 1908 flood, south side of Missouri River across from Anaconda Smelter at Black Eagle Falls. PHOTO COURTESY OF ANACONDA CO., G.F. DIVISION.

was now 15 to 30 percent above normal with very little melt.

A high rate of snow melt began the last few days of May. By June 6 saturated mountain soils and a ripe snow pack were ready to contribute to the rapid response to the heavy precipitaton of June 7 and 8. The stage was set for one of the greatest floods ever in Northwest Montana. Most streams and rivers were flowing to capacity when the heavy rains began.

The floods of 1964 struck parts of the Hudson Bay, Missouri and upper Columbia River Basins. The area of the most severe flooding extended north along the Continental Divide from Helena to southern Alberta, Canada.

The first indication of what was to come was the rapid rise on the smaller streams near the front range of the Rockies. The mostly treeless areas of Glacier National Park allowed the heavy rainfall to reach the streams quickly causing very rapid rises. The streams rose slowly during the day of June 7, but by midnight, the streams flowing into the Belly and St. Mary's Rivers began rising more rapidly and in the next 12 hours would rise five to six feet. Bridges, trees, rocks or anything in the path of the rushing waters were soon part of the rampaging streams. By 4 p.m. on June 8 the streams had reached their peak and were receding slowly.

Severe flooding in the upper Columbia River basin was confined to the upper reaches of the Blackfoot and Flathead River drainage areas. Water was a foot deep in the east end of Lincoln as Landers Fork roared into the valley.

The Flathead River basin upstream from Flathead Lake had the most severe flooding of modern times. All main bridges upstream from Columbia Falls were washed out or rendered unusable. The Middle Fork of the Flathead River caused extensive damage in the narrow valley along the southern boundary of Glacier National Park. More than 15 miles of U.S. Highway 2 disappeared along Bear Creek, an eastern tributary of the Middle Fork. The Middle Fork of the Flathead River had a peak flow of about 140,000 cubic feet per second (cfs) at West Glacier. The 140,000 cfs at West Glacier was almost 60,000 cfs greater than the record peak flow at Plains—below the confluence of the Clark Fork and Flathead Rivers. The flow was so great on the Middle Fork of the Flathead that a rocky canyon downstream from West Glacier constricted the flow and for a time part of the Middle Fork actually flowed upstream into Lake McDonald.

Most of the flow on the South Fork of the Flathead River was regulated at Hungry Horse Dam. As the flood waters flowed into Hungry Horse the discharge from the dam was decreased to a minimum. The flood waters were stored in the reservoir along with hundreds of trees and other debris as widespread severe flooding caused damage upstream from the dam. Unlike Gibson Dam, an irrigation dam, Hungry Horse Dam was constructed as a hydro, recreation and flood control structure.

Downstream from the Three Forks of the Flathead River the peak flow was 176,000 cfs. Without Hungry Horse Dam the peak flow would have been an astounding 245,000 cfs. As the flood waters collected at Columbia Falls, about 50 homes were destroyed. More than 350 homes were flooded in the Days Acres and Evergreen areas east of Kalispell. Lowland flooding from Columbia Falls to Flathead Lake totalled approximately 25,000 acres.

Flooding in the Missouri River drainage began quickly along the foothills. The towns of Augusta, Choteau and Valier experienced flooding during the day of June 8 and about the same time as water reached its peak over the parapet walls of Gibson Dam. At 7:30 p.m., the peak discharge passed through Augusta and Choteau.

Elk Creek (locally called South Fork of the Sun River) inundated much of Augusta. Thirty-four homes and 17 business establishments were damaged as water three feet deep poured through town.

In Choteau, floodwaters from the Teton River and a tributary, Spring Creek, combined to cause a hasty evacuation of the entire town of nearly 2,000 residents. Water up to six feet deep damaged 640 homes and businesses.

Meanwhile at Gibson Dam the water had been going over the parapet walls until about 10 a.m. Tuesday June 9. The lake elevation was above the top of the glory hole on Gibson Dam until early in the morning of June 10. The peak flow on the Sun River at Simms occurred between 6 and 10 a.m. on Tuesday June 9. Because of this, many people mistakenly estimated the water over Gibson Dam began on Sunday June 7. The peak at Simms was the result of local inflow into the Sun River below Gibson Dam. A second, and lower peak, passed Simms later in the day of June 9, the result of water flowing over the parapet at Gibson Dam. The flood waters moved rapidly downstream and the peak passed Vaughn at 6 p.m. on Tuesday June 9. As the flood waters passed Vaughn, a peak discharge of 53,500 cfs was measured. This compared to a flow of 17,900 cfs during the "great flood" of 1953. The peak flow on the Sun River reached Great Falls' 14th Street Bridge at 12:45 a.m. June 10. The river at Great Falls had exceeded flood stage before midnight on June 8. A slow rise was noted on the river until about 7 p.m. on June 9, at which time a very rapid rise was observed.

Day in and day out, the Missouri River at Great Falls caused a backwater on the Sun River, because of a greater flow. On June 9 and 10 the Sun River caused the Missouri River to back up and cause considerable flooding in the Meadowlark Golf Course and the Country Club Addition. The most extensive flooding occurred from Simms to Great Falls. The town of Sun River was completely flooded as was a new suburban area near Vaughn.

Nearly 3,000 persons were evacuated from West Great Falls, as water 10-12 feet deep spread over the area. Twenty-four businesses and 681 homes sustained damage. The severe flooding of the Sun River caused millions of dollars damage, but because of advance warnings, no lives were lost.

Farther north on some tributaries to the Marias River the opposite was true. The failure of two irrigation dams caused widespread and severe flooding as well as loss of life.

Swift Dam on Birch Creek released more then 30,000 acre feet of water. Indirect measurements downstream from the dam substantiated reports of a very fast breach of the dam. The Birch Creek Valley presented a scene of vast devastation. All the trees and most of the brush were swept away. A wall of water 20 feet high also destroyed buildings and bridges that stood in its way. In all, 19 persons along Birch Creek lost their lives. Eight were members of one family. The dam on Lower Two Medicine Lake in

Glacier National Park failed and released a flood wave on Two Medicine Creek on June 8. Eight persons escaped the flood crest as they stood on a stranded pick-up, but nine others lost their lives when they were unable to escape the rapidly rising waters.

Although a high flood crest moved downstream as a result of the dam break, the peak discharge on Two Medicine River occurred about three hours earlier.

The Marias River formed from Badger Creek and Two Medicine River, which includes Birch Creek and Cut Bank Creek, caused considerable damage to a steel truss bridge near Valier and to the roadway on U.S. Highway 91 south of Shelby. The flow of the Marias River was then stored in Tiber Reservoir, preventing further flooding downstream.

ANNUAL DISCHARGE RATE
OF MONTANA'S MAJOR RIVERS

Clark Fork	15,500,000 acre feet
Kootenai	10,190,000
Missouri	7,426,000
Yellowstone	9,470,000

Since 1953, major flooding has occurred along the Continental Divide from Helena to Alberta every 11 years. Can we expect another major event in 1986?

▰▰▰▰▰ FORT BENTON ▰▰▰▰▰
FOUGHT THE MISSOURI, 1908

by John G. Lepley

The spring of 1908 was a dry one. In spite of that, a flash cloudburst in April took out the log dam at Hauser Lake on the upper Missouri but created no problems downriver. Then on May 20 it started to rain, a welcome relief to the stockmen who needed grass in their barren pastures. Thirteen inches of snow fell in the mountains and foothills, and May 30-June 1, when two more inches of rain fell across Montana, moisture in the headwaters was very abundant. During the last of May the Missouri's headwaters had received eight inches of moisture, the heaviest rainfall in 28 years.

By June 3 the tributaries were rising rapidly and going over their banks. The Northern Pacific Railroad lost part of its track between Livingston and Bozeman. As the surge continued downstream, four miles of track was lost by the Montana Central near Cascade.

In Great Falls the city's pumping station was under water, the west side of the Sun River was flooded, and the upper end of Belt was inundated by Belt Creek. Sand Coulee mines were also threatened, but the greatest danger was to the power house on Black Eagle Dam. Finally the headgates gave way, taking out the boiler and power house, which caused the

Upper: Fort Benton, 1908, from hill back of town. Bridge is out. Lower: Grand Union and Front Street, 1908. PHOTOS COURTESY OF JOHN G. LEPLEY.

smelter to lose its energy supply and allowed a large volume of water from the dam to flow downstream.

Highwood reported on June 10 that it had rained every day for three weeks and in May alone 4.04 inches had fallen. The Teton River was at flood stage, too, taking out all bridge approaches in Chouteau County. People living in the river town of Fort Benton sat watching and waiting.

Since the days of the fur fort in the 1840s and 1850s the settlers had lived and worked along the banks of the Missouri. The fur traders came first, using it to haul trade goods to the Indians and mountain men and in the spring to return hides and furs to St. Louis. By 1860 Pierre Chouteau had brought the steamboat all the way to Fort Benton. The following year, with the discovery of gold in Grasshopper Gulch, the Missouri became the main road West. Fort Benton's Front Street grew up with the river on one side and the stores and warehouses of the merchant princes on the other.

Those "glory" days had faded by 1908, and the trading center of the Northwest had become a sleepy, quiet ranching and farming community. Since 1888 when James J. Hill's railroad arrived, Fort Benton's bustling population, which grew to three or four thousand each spring with the coming of the boats, had dropped to 1,500 permanent residents.

The talk there during the days of early June 1908 was whether the water would get as high as it had in 1876. In that year water crept into town but since there were so few homes and businesses at that time, there was little concern. With the building boom of the 1880s, however, many fine brick dwellings and businesses had been built, as well as a bridge which spanned the river in the middle of town. Therefore, high water in 1908 was of far more concern to the citizenry.

Over the next three days the river continued to rise. By then it was bank-full and covered the low ground opposite the town. By Friday night June 5 it was rising six inches per hour.

Mayor Stranahan had crews of volunteers working day and night sand-bagging the pump station and thus saving Fort Benton's water supply.

Through other low areas along the old levee came water which filled the T.C. Power warehouse and the City Hall. At dawn the next day it was three feet deep along Front Street and was lapping at the last step into the Grand Union Hotel. By mid-morning water was flowing along Front Street as if it were part of the river. At the Court House, three streets back, the water was a good five feet deep. The old river channel was located on that street; the water therefore came not over the levee but along the old channel in back of the fairgrounds and down through the middle of town.

By then all available boats were in use, rescuing stranded people and taking them to high ground above the city. Horses and wagons also served as rescue vehicles since they were tall enough to avoid the high water in most areas. The people who had been moved to high ground were sheltered in the large mansions on the hill. The Duer, Harris, Overfield and Frields families cared for and prepared meals for the homeless whose children enjoyed an afternoon of boating and rafting in "Montana's Venice." That evening, as darkness settled over the city, music could be heard above the rampaging water as gramophone concerts were provided by those on higher ground.

On that Saturday morning the wooden icebreakers in front of the bridge piers collapsed, allowing debris to pile high against the piers. Water continued to rise until it reached the bridge decking. All afternoon the center pier which supported the 200-foot draw span was being undercut by the current; the span began to lean upstream. At 11:30 p.m. the water caught both sides of the span and broke it into pieces which fell into the raging torrent. The crash echoed all over town. All during Saturday afternoon water continued to flow down Washington and Franklin Streets, then through the side streets to the river.

The light plant was flooded and Fort Benton plunged into darkness on

Saturday night. The residents simply dug out the kerosene lanterns, which they kept handy since power shortages and blackouts frequently occurred in those early days of electric lights. The abandoned fort suffered most. Parts of the remaining walls were used in diking efforts and the remainder was so thoroughly saturated that its deterioration advanced years in only a few hours.

By noon of the next day the water began to recede and the town took stock of the damage. Losses fortunately proved to be limited. Only houses along Franklin and Washington Streets had water over their floors. Two adobe structures on Front Street, the Flanagan Drug Store and the Baker Store, had received extensive damage to their fronts. The wooden sidewalks and fences had been swept away. Destruction of the sidewalks hastened concrete replacements. The levee had held, thanks to government riprap which had been laid at the end of the steamboat era.

The river had been six to eight feet above flood stage, but by Monday all had returned to their homes to clean up. The Grand Union Hotel was open for business, never having had the Missouri within its walls.

With the bridge span gone, a gasoline launch provided service to people south of town. Within a few days Captain Stevens and C.W. Morrison furnished 700 feet of steel cable and a foot bridge was constructed between the bank and the second bridge span. It was 230 feet long and a very precarious crossing! On July 1 a $5,000 contract was let to O.E. Peppard to complete a span replacing the one that was lost. The new one was a stationary span since the need for a draw span had long since passed. The bridge was completed on schedule, November 1, 1908. On July 8 a temporary ferry had been placed in the river to bring vehicles back and forth. The irony of the whole affair was that on August 12 the ferry could not operate. Why? Low water!

The only victim of the flood was a Fort Benton citizen named Peter Bentzen. He was catching driftwood at the head of Roosevelt Island when he fell into the Missouri and was swept to his death.

So ends the only flood of Fort Benton's history. The small town continues to respect the Missouri's power, recalling its days as Montana's Venice.

■■■■■■ MILWAUKEE ■■■■■■
TRESTLE COLLAPSE, 1938
by Warren G. Harding

The crack passenger train of the Chicago, Milwaukee and St. Paul was traveling west toward Miles City on its route between Chicago and Tacoma. It was the air conditioned Olympian, made up of 11 cars and pulled by a steam locomotive. Most of the passengers were sleeping or dozing in their seats. It was just a few minutes past midnight on Sunday, June 19, 1938.

The Milwaukee track walker had just covered his section and noted that Custer Creek, a short creek flowing from the highlands of the north into the Yellowstone River, was virtually dry and that the trestle spanning the gulch of the creek appeared to be in safe condition. At Calypso, Montana, about seven miles west of the mouth of Custer Creek, the station agent made a note on his records that at 12:14 a.m., a light rain was falling. The agent at Saugus, one quarter of a mile east of the creek reported no rain.

At 12:34 a.m., the train dispatcher at Miles City suddenly lost all wire connections east of his station. It was the first hint of the disaster that had taken place at that moment. While the Olympian had been moving westward through the dark at what was thought to have been full speed, a devastating cloudburst was occurring over the drainage of Custer Creek. A tremendous wall of water rushed down the creek and hit the steel and concrete trestle, weakening it to the extent that when the locomotive started to cross, it collapsed under the weight. Some speculated that the bridge had already been swept away before the train reached it.

The speed of the locomotive carried it across the stream where it struck the bank and settled back into the water, pulling the tender, baggage car, two coaches and two tourist sleepers into the flooding stream. The Olympian's brakeman, whose life had been spared, walked back to Saugus where he telephoned for help at 1:10 a.m.

Of the approximately 140 people on board the train 49 lost their lives, and 65 were injured. Recovery of the bodies was very difficult because many were trapped in the submerged cars. The recovery teams worked in unseasonably warm weather with Miles City temperatures well above 90 degrees for several days after the tragedy. The Yellowstone carried bodies as far as Sidney, 130 miles distant.

The collapsed trestle had crossed the gulch formed as Custer Creek cuts its way through the high clay cliffs and foothills on the north bank of the Yellowstone River about 30 miles east of Miles City. At this point, the river runs between the railroad track and U.S. Highway 10, and access was cut off from the south side.

Reporters viewing the scene from the air described it as though some great force had scrambled the train and created every possible hazard for its load of humanity and at the same time selected a spot where aid was almost entirely impossible. The same reporters were able to count only four or five of the 11 cars, with the rest submerged in the muddy pit. There was no sign of the bridge itself. The stream was running 20 feet deep at the crash site the next day. The conductor's records were swept away in the flood.

The crash of the Olympian was the worst rail disaster in the United States since 1925, and the first one in which a paying passenger had lost his life in 20 years. From Helena came the report that this had been the second major catastrophe in the history of Montana railroading. On September 25, 1908, a Northern Pacific passenger train crashed head on into a freight train during a blinding snowstorm, killing 21 passengers. This occurred between Billings and Columbus.

From Roundup, Montana, came reports of heavy rains the same night the Olympian met its fate. Some places surrounding Roundup had hail, while others had rain of cloudburst proportions. Water rushing down coulees washed away the shoulders of Highway 87 and cut into bridge approaches, with some being washed out completely.

Four days later on Wednesday, June 22, another series of cloudbursts and rains began which were at that time the worst in Montana's history. The area around Havre from Laredo on the southwest to Zurich on the east were the hardest hit, although there was flooding at the same time on the Yellowstone, Musselshell and Sun Rivers. At Laredo, 12 miles southwest of Havre, the Emil DeHaan family perished in a flash flood in Gravelly Coulee when a wall of water hit their home and buildings, carrying everything several miles as it poured out of the Bear Paw Mountains. Three other men lost their lives at Gravelly Coulee. Three families were luckier than the DeHaans in that their lives were spared, but they lost their homes and belongings.

More than five inches of rain had fallen in the Gravelly Coulee drainage in one hour just prior to the destructive flash flood. It is difficult to imagine the size and force of this flood which came out of the foothills as a wall of water, traveled more than 10 miles across the relatively flat land below and still had the force to wipe out two miles of Great Northern track at Laredo.

Meanwhile at Havre Bull Hook Creek, an often dry creek which drains part of the runoff between the Bear Paw Mountains and Havre, spread a half mile wide as it rushed through the center of the city during the night. Nearly two inches of rain fell there within an hour, and property damage was estimated at $500,000.

At Zurich another life was lost when a man was caught in a swollen stream. The oldest resident in the town of Chinook said the rain which had occurred Wednesday night was the heaviest in his memory, with two inches falling in an hour and 3.55 inches during the early part of the night. In the Fort Benton area, 27 small bridges were washed out. The Carter ferry was swamped and sunk near the banks of the Missouri River. In the Sun River Valley, irrigation canals were washed out as was a portion of the Great Northern track.

In addition to the track washed out at Laredo, 60 feet near Waco (49 miles east of Billings), and 600 feet near Zurich were also ruined. A rock slide at Belt held the Great Northern train from proceeding for several hours.

• • •

A sluggish, moist, warm southerly flow had been over Montana for a number of days prior to the Olympian disaster. This is a very typical flash flood type of weather pattern, innocent looking with its subtropical moisture and instability. It was unseasonably warm over eastern Montana and had been dry over the entire state the first part of June. By the middle of the month precipitation was increasing in the form of heavy shower activity and thunderstorms. The heavy showers the night of the Olympian crash were quite spotty. Vida, Melstone and Flat Willow all had more than 1.5 inches of rain, while Miles City, a mere 30 miles from Custer Creek, had no precipitation.

■■■■■■■■■ OVER THE TOP ■■■■■■■
AT GIBSON DAM, 1964
by Pat Klick

Pat and Ted Klick farm at Simms in addition to operating the K Bar L Guest Ranch with Ted's parents and brother at the Sun River Canyon. They also have a lower ranch located just below Gibson Dam.

Rain! We could hardly recall so much rain . . . . On the mountain across from us water-filled gullies roared off the slopes. It was Saturday, June 6, 1964. The year of the flood.

Telephone and power were out by Monday morning. The small bridge on Blacktail Creek just below us washed out, one of many such breakups between the canyon and Augusta. A car radio offered us contact with the outside. When it announced flooding in lower regions, we worried about the strength of Gibson Dam—whether it could hold under increasing pressure.

Wild water choked with debris began forcing its way around the south side of the dam, sweeping away the reclamation building and demolishing a small house used for powder storage. We watched, terrified at the ease with which the current broke apart these structures and rushed them on downstream. We stood on ground that shook and rumbled continuously under the water's power. Thunder and lightning crashed over the din of the furious water. Ted stood watch through the night, still afraid the dam might give way. Dam caretaker Blondie Slater and his wife grabbed a tent and escaped to higher ground as water approached their house.

The flood poured over the top of the dam during the night. The children and I hiked up the trail later the next day to take a roll of movie film, finding ourselves struggling through knee-deep torrents on trails that had become creeks.

Almost anticlimactically, the water receded about noon on Tuesday, June 9. Drama and tension were replaced by mess and drudgery—freezers of meat about to spoil, scavenging neighbors with the audacity to use a barge to steal property washing down-river from our ranch; an argument that resulted in our reclaiming at least some of the items.

Days were consumed manning a caterpillar for bridge reconstruction across Blacktail Creek, and blasting to make a road for our eventual re-entry into Augusta. A cable and overhead trolley car offered free-swinging and somewhat heart-stopping rides across the river. Supplied with walkie-talkies by the Forest Service, we talked with others stranded by the catastrophe.

Our ordeal was minimal compared to those who lost families. Yet memories of the foreboding and isolation that we felt during the flood's darkest hours would remain with us.

•   •   •

The amount of water that fell in the Gibson drainage during the flood of June 1964 was so great that even if the dam had been completely empty when the storm began, the water would have overflowed the glory hole and gone over the parapet of the dam. Some estimates are that it would have been filled two and one half times. Built with Bureau of Reclamation funds, the dam was designed for irrigation, *not* flood control.

Gibson Dam is the key structure of the Bureau of Reclamation's Sun River Project, composed of the Greenfield and Fort Shaw Divisions. The Sun River Project utilizes the waters of the Sun River and tributaries by conserving and regulating storage in Gibson, Pishkun and Willow Creek Reservoirs. The watershed area above Gibson is approximately 1,000 square miles, much of it part of the famous Bob Marshall Wilderness Area. Stream runoff from the drainage areas is mainly derived from rain and snow. However, many underground springs contribute to the water supply.

In addition to 10,000 acres on the Fort Shaw Division and 80,000 acres on the Greenfield Division being served by this system, several small private irrigation companies also obtain water from Sun River and its tributaries.

Gibson Dam was completed in 1929 and is a concrete arch structure 195.5 feet high. When full it contains 99,057 acre-feet of water. There are two outlet structures near the base of the dam with an original capacity of 2,000 cubic feet per second, later enlarged to 3,016 cubic feet per second. These valves were designed to allow the normal stream flow to escape. Thus, when the spring runoff begins, this is the maximum water that can be released until the level reaches that of the glory hole spillway located at the north end of the dam. The glory hole has a capacity of 50,000 cubic feet per second and was considered by the designers of the dam to be more than adequate.

It was not until after the crisis was over that the people living in the flooded Sun River Valley realized water had poured over and around Gibson Dam, thus sparing them many hours of additional anxiety.

ST. MARY DELUGED, 1964

by Bob Frauson

It was raining hard at St. Mary Ranger Station. Rangers checked Divide Creek, which was running deep this Sunday afternoon, June 7, 1964. Two weeks before there had been heavy, wet snowfall at St. Mary, and these valley snow depths were only about half of what the surrounding mountains were receiving.

A ranger ditched the water running down the dirt road that led back to the park's district office. It was warm and raining at all elevations, continuing into the evening. One ranger, riding around the area to check, reported trees were coming down Divide Creek, blocking the bridge by St. Mary Lodge. He alerted the park road foreman that a back-hoe was needed to clear the log jam. Park road crewmen were summoned from the Babb area to assist. The ranger then drove to Many Glacier to make emergency plans.

By the time he returned to St. Mary the trees were piling up faster than the crews could remove them. The state highway department moved additional equipment to the bridge. Highway 89 was washing out between St. Mary Lodge and the state highway complex. Barricades were erected to prevent vehicles from driving off the crumbling highway into the turbulent water. St. Mary Lodge staff worked all night trying to keep the ris-

Upper: St. Mary entrance. Boats only! Lower: St. Mary Lodge marooned.
PHOTOS BY BOB FRAUSON.

ing water, which had engulfed the lodge, from entering the basement. They did not succeed.

The ranger and road foreman contacted park headquarters to shuttle a bulldozer from Logan Pass to St. Mary. One ranger, patrolling from the bridge to the highway department complex, noted a state highway department dump truck lying on its side in raging Divide Creek. After contacting the state highway foreman's wife, who believed her husband to be working on the bridge, the park foreman arrived at the accident scene, and belayed the ranger as he waded to the truck. A search of the engulfed cab and the swollen creek were unsuccessful.

Log jams were breaking under the pressure and sudden surges of water raced down the canyon. Thundering rapids and the grinding of boulders accompanied the ever-increasing downpour. Tanks and barrels now were tumbling in the murky water. The highway department's large garage was being undermined and destroyed.

About dawn some of the park's road crew were released to go back to Babb and check on their families. The bulldozer arrived at St. Mary; the driver of the low-boy had tried to load the dozer at Logan Pass without lights. The dozer toppled over and fell on its side. The resourceful driver then drove to Siyeh Bend, loaded another dozer and continued to St. Mary. At one point he had to cross a road washout near Dead Horse Point.

Rangers notified all campers at St. Marys and Rising Sun to seek high ground and remain in their vehicles. All power went out in the valley, eliminating radio and telephone communications. The dozer operator broke the banks of Divide Creek on the park side to take some of the pressure off St. Mary Lodge. Water was deep in the park's St. Mary employee housing area, so all park crews helped evacuate the 55 employees and their families to high ground at the still-intact 1913 ranger station. The water was so deep that the corner of the district office building looked like the bow wave of a steam boat heading upstream. The fire guards' cabin had floated off its foundation, the bracings under the resident trailers had washed away, and the trailers dropped into the muddy water. To evacuate the families in their private cars to the old ranger station, the dozer was pressed into service again, towing each vehicle across the deep, flooded channel below the old ranger station. The water was up to the door handles of the passenger vehicles and they tended to float. Small children laughed and cried while being towed through the deep water. The women and children took over the two-story, log ranger station, and the men and boys sought cover from the rain in the barn and fire cache.

The bulldozer was used to make a reconnaissance of the area and rangers were able to make voice contact with the campers at St. Mary Campground by shouting over the high water that separated them. St. Mary Lake level was so high that it was flowing over the Going-to-the-Sun Road east of the heavy rock bridge which had weathered the flood.

Tuesday morning rain had stopped so the rangers were able to wade back to the Divide Creek bridge and contact the St. Mary Lodge area which had received devastating damage from the flood and log jams. An emergency phone was installed half way up the Hudson Bay Divide on Highway 89. The rangers contacted the Civil Defense Director of Glacier County for helicopters and a nurse to give typhoid shots for all the people in the valley. The nurse then flew to Many Glacier to complete the immunizations. Though there were road wash-outs between Babb and Many Glacier, Sherburne Dam did not burst due to wise management on releasing flood waters by the local Bureau of Reclamation supervisor. On Thursday the body of the state highway road foreman was found between the

Divide Creek bridge and St. Mary River. There were more than 30 drownings on the Blackfoot Reservation.

There had been no contact with park headquarters since Sunday. All water supplies on the east side were destroyed, road washouts were common, the Two Medicine Dam had gone out, trail bridges on the east side of the park were gone, Highway 2 had washed out, and the Great Northern Railroad had wash-outs. Other national parks sent engineers, plumbers and maintenance people to help the park recover. The military sent 16 helicopters to shuttle crews and materials to inaccessible places. One helicopter crashed on Boulder Ridge but the pilot and chief engineer of the hotel company were able to bushwack back to Many Glacier. The boat concessioner's crafts in winter storage sheds adjacent to the flooded lakes floated up and crushed the roofs of the boat houses. The Going-to-the-Sun Road was quickly repaired and took Highway 2 non-commercial traffic all summer. The railroad made temporary repairs and ran its first train 18 days after the flood.

•   •   •

A repeat flood occurred 11 years later on the east front on June 21, 1975. The flood was not as devastating as the 1964 flood because the earlier experience had taught some safety precautions.

Flathead Valley under flood waters, airport vicinity, 1964. PHOTO COURTESY OF HUNGRY HORSE NEWS.

Avalanche! Glacier's Goat Lick Slide

by Dave Panebaker

Editor's Note:

The Goat Lick Avalanche on Highway 2 near Glacier Park occurred during February, 1979. Though one could probably write an entire book on the avalanche history of this road, the Goat Lick incident was one of the more serious and colorful. Area residents and sightseers thronged to observe close-up one of winter's more frightening and unpredictable aspects. Park rangers at the slide area explained conditions and forces involved in the loss of the bridge.

An incident report written by ranger Dave Panebaker of Walton Station follows. It offers a blow-by-blow account involving a Coca Cola truck which plowed into the avalanche before officials had even received word that the Goat Lick Bridge was torn out and the highway totally impassable.

• • •

At 0715 Bob Joyce contacted me at the Walton Ranger station about a coke truck stuck in an avalanche blocking Hwy. 2 at MP (Mile Post) 181.3. . . .

At 0745 I sent a blind radio call advising that Hwy. 2 was closed 3/4 mile east of Walton by an avalanche and that a coke truck was stuck in it.

At 0815 we put up the "road closed" between Essex and East Glacier at the chain-up area north of Essex Jct. Three semi-drivers were at the area and they agreed to stop traffic there. At 0845 Bob Joyce (the coke employee) and I started walking the road toward the bridge to check for other avalanches and to see if any vehicles were stuck between them. It was raining and very slippery walking on the ice-covered road. We noticed two small sluffs in the west lane across from the North Goat Lick parking area.

At 0917 we reached the bridge area and noticed a large avalanche across the road, approximately 30-40 feet deep. From a distance we thought the avalanche completely covered the bridge; as we walked closer we observed that the bridge was gone, and that all the snow was in the road on the south side of the gully. I called this information to Janet Panebaker at the Walton [Station] who relayed it to Park Headquarters. I also called for road barricades and road closed signs for the Essex Jct. We could not see any portion of the bridge structure in the run-out area. One finger of the deposition zone crossed the river; however there appeared to be no damming behind it. I radioed Walton that I was going to quickly cross the slide to see if any vehicles were on the other side. The area had a very strong odor of fresh sap due to all the matchstick timber incorporated with the avalanche. The avalanche snow was very wet and in large loose

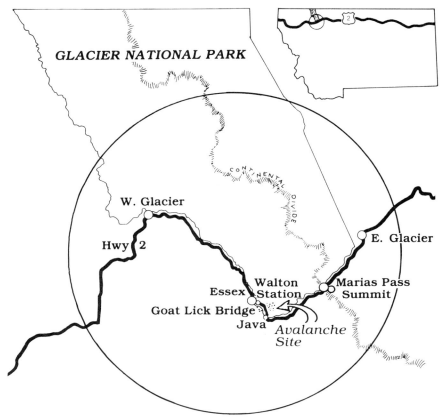

balls and chunks. No vehicles or other avalanches were observed south of
the slide toward Java. I took about 20, 35 mm color slides, Kodachrome
64, of the slide area. It was a constant rain, very unstable conditions, so we
quickly returned to the other side of the slide, keeping radio contact with
Walton during the crossing. At about 0935 the two Nyack plows reached
the bridge site.

They sanded the area, turned around, and gave us a ride to the coke
truck avalanche which they had cleared for one lane traffic. The area was
cleared of all vehicles and people and Hwy. 2 was closed at the Essex Jct.
At 1031 Jim Burnett (East Glacier R.S.) reported that "road closed" signs
were up at Summit and East Glacier.

Due to the high avalanche danger it was decided that no one would be
permitted to go up and view the slide. At 1050 Claude Tesmer arrived
with road barricades and "road closed" signs. The N.P.S. rotary plow arrived shortly. Since there was no work for it along the highway in the park
since the bridge was out, it cleaned out the Walton Ranger Station parking
area and returned to West Glacier. On the way back it cleaned up the
slides at Blue Cut.

At approximately 1110 Art Sedlack arrived with the West Lake avalanche kit [containing probes, ropes, shovels, flashlights, etc.] and 4
Skaadis [electronic devices for locating avalanche victims]. He mentioned

PHOTOS BY DAVE PANEBAKER.

Upper: Goat Lick scenic drive terminated abruptly when an avalanche demolished a reinforced concrete bridge. Lower: Highway 2 is notorious for avalanches. This is another view of the Goat Lick slide.

that on the way down, Blue Cut was only one lane wide due to avalanches. During the remainder of the day someone was always stationed at the Essex Jct. to stop traffic. At about 1230 the highway department brought down its front-end loader from Pinnacle and put up a snow barricade across Hwy. 2 just south of the Walton R.S. . . .

Bob Frauson [Hudson Bay District Ranger] was working with the railroad crews clearing slides across the tracks along Snowslip Mountain. He finally convinced Division Superintendent Hagan in Havre that the railroad shouldn't be clearing the avalanches across the tracks due to the high danger of more slides. BN crews pulled out of the area. The St. Marys' avalanche kit was stored at the Summit Hwy. Department garage.

At 1610 Al Trulock flew in with pilot Jim Kruger in helicopter 65J and landed in the chainup area north of Essex Jct. They picked me up and we flew the highway to make sure no vehicles were stranded between the avalanches and to determine the extent of avalanche damage to the Goat Lick Bridge, railroad tracks and highway. We located the Goat Lick Bridge structure on the river flood plain south of the main avalanche deposition area. The metal structure appeared to be intact. There were no signs of any vehicles in the avalanche debris. We counted 11 avalanches across the railroad tracks and snow sheds and three across Hwy. 2 east of Java.

The only slides on the road inside the park were the coke truck slide, two sluffs by the North Goat Lick parking area, and the main Goat Lick slide which removed the bridge. A state plow was stuck off the road near the microwave tower. It was abandoned between two slides blocking the highway. . . . Two large slides were observed along the Middle Fork south of Bear Creek on east facing slopes of Java Mtn. It appeared that most of the avalanches started as point avalanches and then slab avalanches were triggered along the adjacent slopes. Low clouds and rain prevented us from really seeing into the high starting zones. Most avalanches appeared to have low starting zones which could relate to the freezing level on the mountains. It appeared that only 30 percent of the slope area slid on the bridge avalanche. The bridge avalanche appeared to be fed from three chute areas.

When It's Springtime in the Rockies: Two Unusually Severe Storms

by Warren G. Harding

The spring of 1903 had been unusually dry east of the Continental Divide in Montana, and stockmen were still feeding hay in the middle of May because the grass had been so slow to start on the range. The condition of livestock was generally poor. The Great Falls Tribune reported in its May 16, 1903 issue that due to the drought many cattle and sheep were dying for lack of water in the Fort Benton area. Although people were still talking about the tragic Turtle Mountain slide which killed more than 75 people at the mining town of Frank, Alberta, the weather was the news of the day.

The May 16, 1903 Great Falls Tribune carried the following news item: GOOD WEATHER NOW ASSURED—Special to the Tribune, Browning, Montana, May 15, 1903. "The Climatic Regulator for the Blackfoot Indians, John Night Gun, who regulates the weather for the Blackfoot Indian Tribe, came to Browning today with a headgear of feathers, which is to attract the rain-laden clouds. On his left cheek bone was painted an eagle sending forth the lightning flashes, while his noble brow was painted fiery red which is to call forth the sun and warm days. John says all this is on the way now, and the reservation folks are glad."

The Tribune also printed the official weather forecast for Montana, issued May 15, 1903, from Washington, D.C. by the U.S. Weather Bureau, and transmitted by telegraph. The forecast called for "Showers Saturday and probably Sunday, cooler Saturday and in extreme southeast portion Sunday."

By Sunday morning, May 17, 1903, a major spring storm had developed over Montana. The news from Havre was that it was raining there, but that a blizzard was raging 50 miles to the west. Main line trains were delayed. Other stories from around Great Falls told of the concern that there would be heavy loss of livestock from the heavy snow and strong wind. It was noted in the Tribune that church attendance in Great Falls had been very light on Sunday.

As the reports of the storm continued to reach the Great Falls Tribune, it was evident that the most severe blizzard conditions were to be found at higher elevations where the rain had changed to snow much earlier. It appeared to be centered over Teton County, and extended south and east to the Little Belt and Big Belt mountains, west to the Rockies, and north to the Canadian border. This area comprises the major portion of what is now called the Northwest Chinook Zone by the National Weather Service. The storm raged for 48 hours. Because the ground was warm when the storm began, the snow became very heavy and wet. A report from Teton County said the wind was so severe it was impossible to describe. Livestock was found dead along all train right-of-ways with the greatest number between Havre and Browning.

Once the storm subsided, ranchers started looking for their livestock. At that time more sheep were raised than today. Figures on the numbers of livestock lost from the storm were not available, but from the details of individual losses, it appears to have been large. One Tribune report told of 30 cows being found in one drift near Choteau. David Davies of Vaughn found eight of his yearling steers dead in his corral on Monday morning despite good protection. Hans Olsen of Simms thought he had lost his entire herd of cattle, but the next morning when the storm abated slightly, he found his milk cow had fought its way back to the barn and was standing behind a board fence. Reports taken from the Great Falls Tribune and accounts from early day pioneers tell of large numbers of cattle and sheep dead under drifts along cutbanks and in fence corners.

Reverend Van Orsdel, the pioneer Methodist minister commonly known as "Brother Van," was travelling between Geyser and Belt Sunday in the storm. Eight miles from Geyser he became stuck in a 15 foot drift from which he was able to free himself and his team. The next large drift brought him to a halt, and he was forced to leave his team of horses and walk back to Geyser where he arrived utterly exhausted. He was 54 years old at the time.

After the storm had cleared, the Helena weather office rated it as the heaviest general snow over Montana so late in the year in weather record history. However, measuring precipitation and snow depths accurately in this type of storm is impossible due to the wind; the rain measurement is more accurate than the snow recording. The weather station at Great Falls recorded 4.5 inches of precipitation which began as rain and then changed to snow. If this amount of precipitation is translated to inches of snow at a normal rate of 10 to one, there would have been 45 inches of snow on the level west of Great Falls where the storm began as snow. However, with the ground warm and temperatures above freezing at the onset of precipitation, some downward correction of snow depth should be made. Reports of 10 to 20 foot drifts are logical when the extreme wind speeds are considered. In 1903 with far fewer fences, buildings and trees, the wind carried the snow many miles without meeting any obstacles. The livestock drifted with the wind.

It should be remembered that this storm occurred at the time of year when lilacs are ready to burst into bloom, the leaves are coming out on the trees, and people are planting their gardens. The Crabtree family, who lived along the Missouri near Cascade, recalled having had lettuce and radishes prior to the storm. The small song birds had arrived, and the Tribune reported that following the storm many small birds were found dead in the snow around the city.

Despite the hardships and losses caused by this storm, the moisture which covered most of the state was welcome everywhere. John Night Gun, the climatic regulator of the Blackfoot tribe, probably had received a little more than he had ordered, but no doubt he felt satisfied.

Sixty-six years later eastern Montana had just recorded the longest and coldest winter on record. April, 1969 was the first month with above normal temperatures since the previous November. On the 24th of April, 1969 the following unseasonably warm afternoon temperatures were recorded over southeast Montana: Broadus, 84 degrees; Powderville, 85 degrees; Mildred, 88 degrees. While eastern Montana basked in these temperatures, a Pacific weather system was approaching the state. After leaving small amounts of precipitation in the west, it stalled and intensified over southeast Montana and became one of the most intense storms of modern record.

The storm began as rain, then changed to freezing rain and then to snow. Livestock was first drenched, then chilled to the bone as the strong wind developed and the wet snow plastered the animals. Surveys estimated the losses of livestock at approximately 100,000 animals.

The ice and heavy, wet snow brought communication and power lines down in a short time, and communication lines into Broadus were out for 10 days. Full telephone and electric service were not restored to some rural areas for more than a month. Losses to stockmen and the utility companies ran into millions of dollars. The hardest hit was the southern portion of the southeastern Montana zone, with Powder River County suffering the most severe blizzard conditions.

Determining the snow on the level for comparative purposes is again difficult in a storm of this intensity. Broadus received 2.04 inches of precipitation; Sonnet, west of Broadus, reported 32 inches of snow on the ground on the 26th of April; Colstrip had 4.72 inches of precipitation and reported 14 inches of snow on the ground. One survey team was told of 25-

foot drifts, which is reasonable in view of the extreme winds and long distances before the snow would pile up over a building or other obstruction. The temperature hovered near freezing during this storm.

METEOROLOGICAL EXPLANATION

What conditions cause these violent storms following above normal and even record breaking high temperatures? The abrupt ending of the mountains and the sprawling plains on the east slopes of the Rockies from Alberta to Colorado are conducive to storm development. The first stage in the development of violent spring storms occurs when a ridge of warm air settles in over the Midwest, the Dakotas and Montana. This relatively warm air extends from the land surface to the stratosphere. The characteristics of this air mass make it capable of holding great amounts of moisture, which gives it a high potential for heavy precipitation.

While the warm air has been settling over the plains, a cold upper trough has developed over the Pacific Ocean, extending from the Gulf of Alaska to the California coast. When this cold air mass begins to move eastward, its leading edge produces a Pacific cold front. While this Pacific front and the following cold air approach the Continental Divide, the warm air flow from the south into the Dakotas and Montana increases, resulting in unseasonably warm temperatures. Moisture from the Midwest and the Gulf of Mexico continues to increase in the warm air.

Meanwhile, as the cold air mass and the associated cold upper trough advance eastward, the jet stream shifts to a position flowing northeast from California to eastern Montana. When the cold upper trough spills over the Rockies onto the plains, it is blocked from further eastward movement by the combination of the jet stream and the ridge of warm moist air. The cold air begins to swirl cyclonically (counter-clockwise) forming an upper vortex. An intense surface low (area of extremely low pressure) forms under the jet on the edge of the warm ridge to the east of the upper vortex. A major spring storm is underway.

No two spring storms are identical. They vary in precipitation amounts, area covered, temperature and wind speeds. The wind speed is the element that can turn heavy snow into a vicious blizzard. There have never been enough wind recording stations to give an exact picture of the wind during such storms as those in 1903 and 1969, but it is common for spring storms east of the divide to have wind speeds of 25 to 40 miles per hour. However, reports indicated that in both the 1903 and 1969 storms, the wind speeds approached 100 miles per hour.

The most vicious blizzard conditions in this type of spring storm are found under the northwest quadrant of the upper vortex. The center of the upper vortex in the 1903 storm was over central Montana, placing the western portion of the Northwest Chinook Zone under the northwest quadrant, creating the most severe conditions in this area. In the 1969 storm the center of the upper vortex was over the Black Hills of South Dakota, placing southeast Montana under the northwest quadrant.

Watch for Waterspouts

by Grayson Cordell

Waterspouts don't come along very often, but when they do, watch out! On July 2, 1971, a large and dramatic waterspout was observed over Medicine Lake in northwestern Montana.

Harlow W. Strandlund had been watching a thunderstorm building from his yard south of the lake. After noticing a peculiar cloud formation build downward from the base of the thunderstorm several times, he went into the house and got the camera. Shorty after returning to the yard the waterspout suddenly formed and he snapped the accompanying photographs. The waterspout was about four miles away.

Several minutes after forming, it seemed to dissipate briefly. During this time it apparently was moving across an island. This temporarily shut off

PHOTOS BY HARLOW W. STRANDLUND

its supply of water and disturbed the flow of air into it. It quickly reformed as it moved back over the water.

Waterspouts are usually tornadoes that occur over water. Rarely, very small ones can be formed from the water upward similar to a dust devil over land. In this country they are most common off the Florida coasts.

At least 100 people viewed the waterspout. It appeared different colors to people on different sides of the lake. Dennis Nelson and his father watched it from a county road also south of the lake. To them it appeared almost white and they do not recall it making any noise.

North of the lake, Don White, the official weather observer in the area for the National Weather Service and manager of the Medicine Lake National Wildlife Refuge, his wife, and several other people watched the waterspout from the refuge headquarters yard. They were about two miles from the funnel, and to them it appeared black and roared like several freight trains. Using an island of known size as a background, he estimated it to be approximately 550 feet in diameter.

After a few minutes, it began to hail heavily and the funnel became obscured from sight. According to White, the hail was up to three inches in diameter and peculiarly shaped. The hailstones were thick in the middle surrounded by a much thinner and flat circle of ice, similar to the shape of a small fried egg.

Later, about 30 dead pelicans and cormorants were found. Most appeared to have been killed by the hail, but one pelican was found stripped of feathers as though it had been plucked.

Estimates of the waterspout's duration vary from more than five minutes to less than 20. It apparently moved slowly toward the southeast and dissipated either as it approached shore or shortly after moving onto land.

It is interesting to note that people on all sides of the lake thought that it was moving toward them. Apparently, it grew larger giving everyone the illusion that it was getting closer. This points out the danger in watching a nearby tornado, for it is frequently difficult to estimate either its direction or speed.

At a campground west of the lake, all the lids on the large garbage cans in the recreation center began popping off a few minutes before the waterspout formed over the lake. This was witnessed by many campers who had taken shelter in the building from the threatening storm. Lids popped off the cans because of a sudden drop in the air pressure and probably occurred as that portion of the cloud which later produced the water spout moved over them.

Tornadoes are not a common occurence in Montana, and of course, waterspouts are much more rare. At the time it was thought to be the first recorded waterspout in the state, but files at the refuge headquarters produced an old picture of a very small one on July 22, 1935. Nothing is known about that storm. These two waterspouts are the only ones known to have occured in Montana.

Montana Twister

by Grayson Cordell

Montana has experienced four killer tornadoes this century, killing five people. Two people were killed in Mineral County in 1923, another near Froid in 1946, one at Three Forks in 1948 and the last was at Wibaux in 1952.

Since Montana tornadoes are rare, few of us have ever seen them. But we do have three or four reported in an average year. In the last 30 years, 75 percent have occurred in June or July. Most of them are small, short-lived and do little or no damage, since most occur over the sparsely populated eastern plains. Montana has never had a tornado classified as violent.

Exactly what are they and why do they occur?

Although they are the smallest of nature's violent storms, tornadoes are the most destructive locally. Tornadoes are usually defined as violent, rotating columns of air in contact with the ground. The lower portions are almost always visible as funnels hanging from the parent cloud, usually a large thunderstorm. The funnel may vary in shape from a thin rope-like cloud to a thick mass of black clouds touching the ground. Often the funnel skips along the ground moving erratically, but generally in a north-east direction. The speed can vary from almost stationary up to 70 m.p.h. in extreme cases.

A tornado that does not reach the ground is called a funnel cloud. Whenever one moves over water, it is known as a waterspout. The air in practically all tornadoes rotates in a counter-clockwise direction.

Winds in weak tornadoes are estimated at about 100 m.p.h. or less; in violent tornadoes winds exceed 200 m.p.h. or even 300 m.p.h. Wind measuring instruments are usually blown away in tornado conditions. Whenever they do remain in operation there is always the question of whether or not they received the storm's full force. The highest wind value ever recorded was 151 m.p.h. at Tecumseh, Michigan in 1965 along the southern edge of a three-mile-wide damage path.

Air pressure in large tornadoes can be as much as 10 percent or more lower than in the area just outside the funnel. Thus, damage by a tornado is increased because higher pressure inside buildings may push walls and roofs outward, enabling the wind to carry them off as connections weaken. Weaker buildings can give the appearance of literally exploding. Only buildings of reinforced concrete or structural steel escape serious damage.

All severe thunderstorms can produce heavy rain, large hail and strong, damaging winds. Such conditions also may accompany a tornado, but include rotating rather than straight-line winds. But why one severe thunderstorm will spawn a tornado while tens of others do not is not understood.

Forecasters can be certain, though, that when the following conditions exist, severe thunderstorms and tornadoes are possible:

1 . Very unstable air through a great depth of the atmosphere allowing a rapid vertical turning over of air columns.

2 . Warm and moist air at the low levels. To us, it is sultry or muggy air.

3 . The presence of dry air in the middle levels of the atmosphere above the moist layer. Without this dry layer, thunderstorms are likely to be less serious.

4 . Winds increasing greatly with height. Air at these high levels also should be cold and dry.

5 . Some mechanism to trigger the overturning of the atmosphere such as intense heating by the sun or an approaching weather system containing colder air.

Severe thunderstorms do not occur randomly when these conditions are met. Instead they form in lines, normally along boundaries of converging winds or cold fronts.

The National Severe Storm Forecast Center in Kansas City, an office of the National Weather Service, issues "Tornado Watches" one to seven hours in advance.

A "Tornado Watch" identifies a relatively large area (usually about 140 miles wide by 200 miles long) where a tornado *might* occur. The watch only indicates areas of greatest probability and tells the public to remain alert for further advisories.

A "Tornado Warning" is not issued until a tornado has been signed or picked up by radar. If you should ever be in an area where a warning is issued, act immediately to protect yourself and family. Do not confuse the terms "watch" and "warning!"

As a tornado approaches, the sky may become a seething, boiling mass of clouds that change colors. The sound is comparable to the roaring of many freight trains.

While tornadoes can be killers, there are ways to protect yourself. At home, stay away from windows and seek shelter in the lowest part of the house under heavy furniture, and protect your head. Interior hallways or large buildings are safest. If caught in the open, lie flat in a ditch, ravine or culvert with your hands protecting your head.

Mobile homes and cars are not safe! In the 1979 Wichita Falls, Texas tornado, 25 of the 47 victims died trying to outrun the tornado in their cars. Ten of 11 victims in nearby Vernon were in cars. Mobile home occupants in a Wichita Falls mobile home park evacuated and sought shelter in large buildings. Ninety-three homes were destroyed and nearly the entire mobile home park, but not a life was lost.

An Extraordinary Wind: The Day Gov. Nutter's Plane Went Down

by Warren G. Harding

Thursday, January 25, 1962, at approximately 3:30 p.m., a Montana Air National Guard C-47 crashed about eight miles southwest of the town of Wolf Creek, killing Montana's governor, Donald P. Nutter. The group was enroute from Helena to Cut Bank where the governor was to address the Highway 2 Association, the Montana Barley Growers and the Cut Bank Chamber of Commerce. Also killed were his executive secretary, Dennis B. Gordon of Billings; Edward G. Wren, a rancher from Cascade and the state agricultural commissioner; Major Clifford E. Hanson, pilot from Great Falls who was a supervising air traffic controller with the FAA; Major Joseph R. Devine, copilot from Great Falls; and Master Sergeant Charles W. Ballard, flight engineer, also from Great Falls.

Thursday morning, unusually strong southwesterly to westerly winds had developed over the Continental Divide and swept eastward across the plains in response to an intense surface low moving across Alberta into Saskatchewan and an associated Pacific cold front crossing the state. Another contributor to strong westerly surface winds was the surface high present over the Great Basin. This weather pattern is noted for its severe turbulence within 3,000 feet of the terrain. The winds at the 10,000-foot level that day were generally in the 60 to 80 m.p.h. range as they crossed the Continental Divide and settled into the mountain valleys along the east slopes of the Rockies.

Although the most severe turbulence and surface winds are generally found in the frontal zone, on this day the strong cold advection caused very turbulent conditions over the mountains many hours after the front had passed. When the front moved through the Augusta-Fairfield-Choteau area earlier in the day, the Sun River REA reported 66 large poles were snapped off. The poles were 2 feet in diameter at their bases, and 1 foot in diameter at their tops. They were set 6½ feet in the ground, and were carrying a three phase set of lines. Fuller-Webb, the Minute Man Missile contractor, recorded gusts to 108 m.p.h. on its anemometer near Choteau, and the Pincer Creek weather station, east of Crow's Nest Pass in Alberta, recorded the same.

Pilot reports that day gave the picture of 2,000 feet per minute up and down drafts over the mountains as well as moderate to severe turbulence in the vicinity of the mountains. The terrain-induced turbulence at lower levels that day was in contrast to reports of smooth air above 12,000 feet mean sea level. This contrast is not unusual in this type of wind pattern.

Dearborn residents reported that day to be the windiest they had ever observed, while residents of the Wolf Creek Canyon area estimated the winds to be near 100 m.p.h. On the other hand, the Great Falls airport wind showed gusts of only 53 m.p.h.

Harold Farrell of Missoula, a logger working the Wolf Creek area, witnessed the final descent of the C-47 under the clouds and its subsequent crash into the mountainside. He reported good visibility, no precipitation, and a cloud deck between 8,000 and 10,000 feet. With the exception of the strong winds, the weather was good.

The initial investigation revealed that the outer portion of the right wing was missing. After two days of searching, the 22-foot section was found approximately one mile south along the flight path. This section had separated from the plane in flight and fluttered to the ground completely intact with no apparent damage. Even the trees among which it landed showed little trace of the wing's descent.

The investigative report indicated metal fatigue in the wing, coupled with turbulence, caused the wing to separate from the plane and the crash to occur.

No Snow: Great Falls' Winterless Winter

by Grace D. Harding

On April 1, 1926, Great Falls was the scene of a most unusual celebration. Stores were closed, school children were dismissed and the mayor issued a proclamation urging all citizens to support and participate in the big event. Photographers came from New York City to film the festivities so that the rest of the United States could witness the big day.

The reason for the celebration? Great Falls and much of the state surrounding it had just enjoyed a winter during which there was no bad weather. The people called it the winterless winter. Records revealed that the mean temperature at Great Falls for the winter season had been warmer than Louisville, Kentucky; Kansas City, Missouri; Boise, Idaho; Salt Lake City, Utah; Denver, Colorado; Washington, D.C.; Baltimore, Maryland; Winnemucca, Nevada; and Atlantic City, New Jersey.

It was at a meeting of the Advertising Club that the idea was suggested by Vincent C. Kelley—let the rest of the world know that Montana was not the frigid, undesirable place in the winter that so many thought it to be. Plans were made to have a Straw Hat Parade on April Fool's Day with two goals in mind: fun for the people and advertising for the state. Mr. Kelley was appointed chairman of the committee to plan and organize the big parade.

Mr. Will Steege, manager of the Liberty Theater, immediately made contact with the Pathe News Company to ask if they would come to photograph the celebration. Before television and the news coverage that is now taken for granted, the Pathe News Company, with the 9,000 theaters which subscribed to its service, provided visual news coverage to movie patrons. It was by this method that the Advertising Club planned to inform the rest of the country of the mild Great Falls climate. When these arrangements were complete, the committee went into action.

110

Don't snow on our parade! Great Falls bathing beauties found their act threatened by the only storm of the season. PHOTO FROM FLOYD P. KIMMITT FILES.

Invitations to take part in the parade were issued to all groups, organizations, business firms, schools and any individual who would care to come as a clown or other specialty number.

The governor, J.E. Erickson, was invited, and his plans were made to come from Helena on the train arriving at 1:15 p.m., just in time to lead the parade, which was to begin at 1:30 p.m. Mr. Frank Brown of the Great Falls Meat Company was chosen as marshall.

Preparations proceeded with great enthusiasm all over the city. The first estimate was that 1,500 school children would take part, but the final number was close to 3,000. Each school had its own banner and slogan, with many students also carrying their own personal banners. Floats were prepared, and the municipal band and the Eagles drum and bugle corps were practicing for the big day. The rumor that Strain Brothers and The Paris, department stores on opposite corners of Central Avenue, were planning to pool their talents and sponsor a float ridden by bathing beauties was getting the most attention.

Despite the apparent confidence that Mother Nature would not let them down at this time of joy, some thought was given to the remote possibility that it might storm and be too cold for the Straw Hat Parade. It was decided to parade regardless with a contingency plan. If the unthinkable happened, the parade was to advertise the only winter day of the year. The announcement by the committee said, "If the day of the parade happens to bring a snow flurry, straw hats will be out of order, and overcoats and proper dress advertising the only winter day of the year should be worn. Women should also conform to the winter dress. However, the committee has urged that people witnessing the parade be dressed to conform to the marchers so that the movie cameras will not get an inconsistent picture."

As the day drew near, the weather did cause the celebrants some worry. A major storm moved across the country, causing scores of deaths and heavy damage in the central region of the United States. It continued east and caused much trouble along the seacoast where many ships were tossed about in the Atlantic. Montana had cool weather with wind and some precipitation. The March 29th issue of the Great Falls Tribune published the following: "Stormy weather of last week leaves some doubt as to the kind of weather Great Falls will have Thursday, April 1st." On March 30, 1926, it was reported that freezing weather had struck the Mountain district in the wake of the four-day snow. The storm brought the coldest temperatures of the winter to some Montana points.

March 31st the mayor, H.B. Mitchell, issued a proclamation urging all residents of Great Falls to join in the Straw Hat Parade. Mr. Mitchell proclaimed, "Realizing the deplorable misunderstanding of Montana's winter climate which has long prevailed in many parts of the United States, which, in fact, are less fortunate climatically than the Treasure State, I urge all citizens of Great Falls to participate in the demonstration to be held in the afternoon of April 1st when Great Falls will celebrate the winterless winter of 1925-26.

"Inasmuch as the parade, the focal point of the festival, is to be filmed by a motion picture company and given national publicity on the screen, it is important that we of Great Falls cooperate to the fullest extent. By doing this, we shall not only advertise our city in a way not otherwise to be hoped for, but will do our part to bring to the people of the United States accurate information concerning Montana winter conditions."

The Advertising Club stressed that the celebration was not planned to help local merchants sell straw hats. Everyone was urged to wear last year's straw hat or bonnet.

April 1 did not dawn warm and sunny in Great Falls. In fact, it was rather cool with a high temperature of 29, and a small amount of snow fell during the day, but it only measured .04 of an inch and did very little to dampen the enthusiasm of either the marchers or the spectators. The Tribune reporters said the crowd gleefully demonstrated its happiness over the weather of the last winter which made the Electric City warmer than Louisville, Kentucky.

The parade was said by some to be the greatest and most spectacular that had ever been held in Great Falls. In addition to the 3,000 school children, there were Boy Scouts, Girl Scouts, Campfire Girls, firemen, policemen, civic and fraternal organizations, labor unions, local business floats with the bathing beauties starring in that category, Cree Indians who lived across the Missouri River from the city, and many novelty entries including a dog wearing a straw hat.

The only thing that marred the joy of the day was the failure of Governor Erickson to arrive on time. The train on which he was to have ridden to Great Falls developed engine trouble between Butte and Helena, and he was forced to travel to the celebration by automobile, thus delaying his arrival into Great Falls until 3 p.m. This was in time for him to take part in a ceremony at Gibson Park where Mayor Mitchell presented him with a straw hat. There was also a banquet that evening at the Park Hotel in honor of the governor, at which time he said that it was a grievous disappointment for him to have missed the parade. The governor was represented in the parade by C.B. Power, son of T.C. Power, one of the state's most distinguished pioneers.

All of the activities were photographed by Frank Ward, who was said to be one of the best cameramen of the Pathe News Company. The films were forwarded immediately to New York City from which they were distributed to the 9,000 theaters served by Pathe. The news reel showing the celebration was shown at the Liberty Theater later during the month, giving the viewers a chance to relive the day they would never forget.

•　　•　　•

The statistics which give the picture of the famous winterless winter are very unusual. Strangely enough, no records were broken. It was simply a winter during which there was not even one severe storm. It was described by the Weather Bureau as the most evenly tempered winter since the station had opened 34 years earlier. There were 79 days with maximum temperatures above freezing, 65 days with maximums above 40 degrees, 25 days with maximums above 50 degrees. The maximum was 63 degrees on March 15th. There were 63 days when the mean temperature (the average of the maximum and minimum temperatures) was above 32 degrees. Zero on January 10 was the lowest recording. The mean temperature from December 21, the first day of winter, until the close of March 20, the last day, was 35.9 degrees, which was 9.7 degrees above the normal for that period. The average high temperature was 45.5 degrees and the average low was only 26.4 degrees.

Great Falls was not alone in enjoying a mild winter. The summary for the month of March written and recorded in the official Weather Bureau records for Montana notes, "The months from November, 1925, through March, 1926, inclusive, constitute a remarkable period in Montana weather including its mildest winter, as a whole, on the Weather Bureau records for the state. During this five-month period Havre averaged 10 degrees per day higher than its normal temperature. The precipitation average is lowest on record."

At Glacier Park the mild winter eliminated game feeding usually necessary for park animals. Hay was on hand at several locations, but it was virtually untouched. Unusually few animals were seen because they were able to find feed at higher elevations. Rangers who made a trip into the area of the South Fork of the Flathead River saw deer and elk and reported they were all fat and had fat calves at their sides. Only the coyotes around the park looked thin and gaunt. The lack of snow had been favorable for their prey. The rangers also reported about half the usual amount of snow in the South Fork watershed.

During the winter at the park there had been no blizzards, no deep snow, and no extreme temperatures. The coldest weather of the winter was minus 3 degrees near Belton, which was recorded one day only and was the only temperature below zero registered. Maximum snow at park headquarters was 18 inches which settled to 12 inches and was maintained through January and February. There was very little snow plowing, and most of the roads were open for automobile travel all winter. The road between the headquarters and Kalispell needed plowing only once, and the road between Glacier Park Station and Babb was open all winter, as was the one to Browning.

Snow Eater:
Montana's Chinook Winds

by Grayson Cordell

For perhaps a week or longer winter has held an icy grip on the Montana landscape. Skies have been clear the past few days with ice crystals floating in the bitter cold air. However, recently it has turned cloudy. Winds are light and from the north or east. Suddenly, the wind shifts to southwest or west, the velocity increases rapidly, the temperature jumps upward and the humidity falls abruptly—chinooks!

Montana, Wyoming and Alberta are the real home of the chinook wind, a relatively warm and dry southwest or west wind blowing down the eastern slopes of the Rocky Mountains. It is perhaps winter's most spectacular weather phenomenon in the area. The temperature will rise in a few hours from below zero to well above freezing, with the snow melting rapidly and water running in the gutter.

"Chinook" supposedly is an Indian word meaning "snow-eater." Its capacity for keeping the ground relatively free of snow and modifying the climate of the "chinook" belt was noted by travellers to the region as early as 1787.

The chinook shares its name with an Indian tribe which formerly lived near the mouth of the Columbia River. The term was first applied to a warm southwest wind which blew from "over the Chinook camp" to the Hudson Bay Company trading post at Astoria, Oregon. Use of the term expanded as the adjacent country was settled, finally finding its way into the vocabulary of the early settlers in Montana and surrounding areas. So the term that originally was applied to a warm and moist southwest wind is now used to describe a warm, dry southwest wind east of the Rocky Mountains.

Chinook winds are not confined to the Rocky Mountain region, but occur in other parts of the world as well. These dry downslope winds belong to the family of "foehn" type winds. These warm winds are best developed where long mountain ranges lie at right angles to the prevailing winds which blow in from an ocean.

They are known by a variety of local names. There is the "south foehn" north of the Alps, the "north foehn" south of the Alps, the "koschava" and "ljukas" of Yogoslavia, the "berg wind" of South Africa, the "zonda" and "puelche" of the Andes, and the "northwester" of New Zealand, to name a few.

The foehn wind has been blamed for a variety of illnesses. "Foehn sickness" seems to take on an indefinite form, but generally is associated with a feeling of low spirits, general ill-being and depression. The suicide rate is said to be unusually high during a south foehn. Other symptoms that have been reported are muscular convulsions, headaches, heart palpitation and increased heart disease. Only the south foehn blowing northward down the Alps out of Italy into Switzerland, Austria and Germany seems to cause this strange sickness.

European doctors and scientists have been unsuccessful in their attempts to explain foehn sickness. Whatever the cause, it seems to occur just as often in closed rooms as it does in open exposed areas.

Where does the chinook wind obtain its heat? Meteorologists do not fully understand all the mechanics of a chinook, but do know of several processes that are involved. Chinook air begins over the Pacific Ocean and is rather warm and usually moist. As the air moves eastward toward Montana, it is forced to rise over several mountain ranges, cooling as it rises. If the air is sufficiently moist, moisture condenses and precipitation occurs as the air passes over the mountains. This process of condensation releases heat that has been stored in the moisture-laden air.

Thus, the air is warmer on the east side of the mountains than it was on the west side at the same elevation.

For chinook conditions to exist, weather maps must show a pressure situation that results in a steady flow of air across Montana from the west or southwest. Therefore, the chinook usually begins with a high-pressure system centered to the south of the state, over Utah or Nevada, and a low pressure system from the Pacific moving eastward across the mountains into southern Alberta. Its approach is heralded by high thin clouds gradually thickening and lowering to an altitude of two or three miles. However, instead of continuing to thicken and lower as they would in case of an approaching storm, a chinook arch forms—a characteristic accompanying cloud.

The chinook belt has rather indefinite boundaries and extends from the mountains eastward for perhaps 10 to 150 miles or so—from the Upper Yellowstone Valley above Billings northward into Canada.

Chinooks do occur to the east of this area, but not as frequently. The closer to the mountains, the more frequent the chinooks. Chinooks are still rather common 200 miles east of the mountains, but perhaps only a couple of chinooks in an average winter will reach as far as the northeastern Montana borders.

Chinook winds occur in all seasons, but their effects are most spectacular in winter when bitter cold air invades the state at intervals. Just before the warm air arrives, the cold air becomes very shallow, perhaps only a few hundred feet thick. Thawing occurs on the mountainsides and buttes before the warm air surfaces on the plains. This frequently causes mirages; the mountains take on strange shapes and appear higher than usual when viewed from within the cold air.

As the warm chinook front moves through an area, dramatic temperature rises can occur. A temperature rise of 43 degrees in 15 minutes, from minus six degrees to a balmy 37 degrees, has officially been noted in Havre by the National Weather Service. I once witnessed a rise of 26 degrees in 45 seconds at Havre, from 16 degrees to 42 degrees.

On December 1, 1896, the temperature observer at Kipp, Montana reported a temperature rise of 34 degrees in seven minutes. The observer further reported a total rise of 80 degrees in a few hours and that 30 inches of snow disappeared in one half day. When temperatures have been very cold for a long time and then rise rapidly, a thick layer of frost immediately forms on the ground. Sidewalks and streets become very slick as traffic quickly turns the frost into a layer of ice. This will last until the ground becomes warm enough to prevent the formation of a frost or melt it, perhaps most of a day.

Some think the frost is coming out of the ground. Actually, the frost comes from the air. Even though the air is relatively dry, what moisture there is condenses on the cold ground as frost, simply because the ground is still extremely cold.

Occasionally the chinook front becomes stationary, oscillating back and forth over a few miles. If the cold air returns before the frost has a chance to melt, the ground again turns cold and the ice remains. Later, perhaps the next day, chinook conditions return to form another layer of frost on top of the old. The warm and cold air masses can battle back and forth for a number of days at a time alternately freezing and thawing, building up an ice layer more than an inch thick on roads.

On one occasion Havre experienced four chinooks in five days. The temperature varied from one degree below zero to 50 degrees above with the chinooks lasting from two to 33 hours.

Another less pleasant southwesterly wind occurs over the plains in winter. It is loosely called a "Klondike chinook" among Montana meteorologists. Instead of the air originating over the Pacific and moving into Montana on westerly winds, its origin is in the far north and moves into the state on northerly winds. Although it descends and then blows from the southwest at ground level, it remains cold simply because the air was so cold originally. Temperatures rise only slowly and may never reach above freezing. It is a bothersome chilling wind causing extensive blowing and drifting snow over the plains and is not welcome as is the true chinook.

Glacier Park Mini-Climate

by Bob Frauson

Glacier National Park makes its own weather (micro climate) due to its location straddling the Continental Divide. The predominant weather influence is the flow of moist, warm air from the Pacific which loses heat as it rises over the passes and mountains that make up the west slope of the Continental Divide. Moisture is lost in the lower elevations as rain. Rain turns to snow as the air cools over the mountains. This same cool air then plunges down the eastern slope gaining speed and warming to become a chinook wind.

Cold fronts from the arctic flow down over the east front range from Siberia, Alaska and through Alberta, forcing their way under the warmer Pacific air. This front may be visible as fog or clouds that form at the con-

Spring breaks through at Many Glacier Hotel. PHOTO BY MEL RUDER.

tact point and even lightning may occur from violent frontal clashes. Large arctic fronts tend to spill over the passes (Logan, Marias, etc.) and flow down into western valleys filling these valleys with cold air, which is trapped under the warm overriding air flowing east. This warm air plummets down the east slope as chinooks and can create winds gusting in excess of 100 m.p.h. In such storms it is difficult to keep the rotating cups on anemometers, as they turn so fast, centrifugal force destroys them.

North winds, which are not winds as such, are the result of a constant pressure of chilling air moving south at from five to 10 m.p.h. Elk herds in winter tend to move into these north storms and have been known to move as far as eight miles in one night, leaving the confines of the park.

Cloud formations that signal weather changes are altocirrus clouds (mares' tails) moving in from the west. They usually precede storms from the west. Lenticular clouds (lens shaped) denote high winds from the west. (See chapter on clouds. ed.) These transform into a chinook arch that can extend from horizon to horizon. In fall and winter, clouds can shroud the Continental Divide and its peaks for days on end. At other times hat-like "cap clouds" settle on the major peaks.

It can snow in Glacier Park any month of the year. Sometimes snow closes Logan Pass as early as the second week in July. One can usually count on a snow storm on Logan Pass the third or fourth week of August, followed by a beautiful Indian summer. Snow that falls in the western valleys is likely to be moister than east slope snow. The rate of snowfall is a good indicator of avalanche danger. If it exceeds one inch per hour, winter travelers in mountainous terrain must beware. White-outs or ground blizzards can occur at any time, even many days after a snowfall, when there is a strong wind and loose snow. Orientation is difficult under these conditions. A friend once described the difficulty of skiing in a white-out as like "skiing inside a ping-pong ball."

Snow in the last four years on the east front of the park has been light, accumulations of as little as 74 inches compared to 330 at St. Mary in the late 1960s.

Skirting a big drift early in the season. PHOTO BY MEL RUDER.

Temperature ranges are extreme and can change very rapidly. One may start on an afternoon cross-country ski trip from Hudson Bay Divide to St. Mary (7-plus miles) in 25 below zero weather with beautiful gliding conditions only to have the temperature rise to 45 above with rain. The snow becomes as sticky as mashed potatoes. Temperatures can stay in the minus 25 to minus 35 temperature range for a week or so at a time. It

---

Bob Frauson's
Emergency Auto Kit
The 10 Essentials for All Trips

1. Map
2. Compass
3. Flashlight
4. Extra Clothing
5. Extra Food and Water
6. Sun Glasses
7. Waterproof and Windproof Matches
8. Candle or Fire Starter
9. Pocket Knife
10. First Aid Kit

---

sometimes dips to minus 50. Goats are good barometers of such weather fluctuations. Note their position on the mountain side. If they are high on the slopes, the weather will be good; when they are low, watch out!

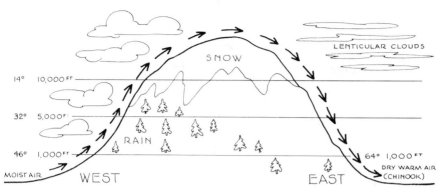

Pacific air, heavy with water, drops rain on western slopes—or snow at higher elevations. Chinooks result as the now-dry air tumbles down the eastern slopes, warming as it descends.

Most of the large lakes in the park are very deep so that a great deal of cooling of the water has to occur before ice can form on the surface. Lake McDonald seldom freezes over in the winter. Yet east-side lakes may freeze over by Thanksgiving. When the large lakes do freeze, one can hear constant booming in the valleys caused by cracking ice. Wind also affects a lake's ice formation. On a calm, cool night the lake may freeze over. Then a wind might spring up to break the ice and send it grinding down the lake. Years ago on just such an occasion an elk herd went out onto St. Mary Lake on a night when the ice was not safe. Coyotes were out on the ice harassing the elk and the herd milled around in a small group. This concentration of the weight caused the ice to break and about 40 elk drowned in a spot no larger than 30 feet by 30 feet.

An old Indian by the name of Alanzo Skunk Cap told me his method of forecasting a winter. He said to watch where the muskrats build their houses. If they are at the edge of the pond, it will be an easy winter. If the houses are in the middle of the pond, it will be a hard winter. Alanzo passed away a few years ago, but when I pass the ponds near his house I always watch where the muskrat houses are.

The Weather of Yellowstone

by Rick Reese

The vast expanse of Yellowstone National Park covers more than two million acres in Montana, Idaho and northwestern Wyoming. Though most of the park is in Wyoming, three of its five entrances are in Montana and the only road open year around links the two Montana communities of Gardiner and Cooke City.

Weather observations were started at the Fort Yellowstone Army post in 1887, the site now occupied by the park service headquarters at Mammoth. Weather observations have been made at Mammoth continuously since that time, providing us with excellent records of weather conditions at a location free from contaminating effects of human activities. Mammoth, however, is not representative of the conditions in Yellowstone National Park generally, since it is at a relatively low altitude by Yellowstone standards and usually much milder than other locations in the park. Reporting stations in the interior of the park at Lake, Canyon, Old Faithful and Lamar give a more accurate picture of weather conditions, and records at these sites have been kept for many years though not as long as for Mammoth.

The 45th parallel of latitude runs through the northernmost portion of the park placing Yellowstone at a point exactly mid-way between the equator and the north pole, far enough north to feel the effects of arctic fronts. But Yellowstone is also far enough west to be affected by winter flows of Pacific air which can bring sudden warming trends and send the mercury soaring. Together, these two influences contribute to the highly variable conditions in the area.

Another factor contributing to weather variations in Yellowstone is altitude. The Continental Divide runs directly through the park and elevations range from 5,282 feet north of Mammoth to 11,358 feet at Eagle Peak, a difference in elevation of more than 6,000 feet.

Extreme variability, then, is perhaps the major theme of Yellowstone weather: variability in weather from place to place in the park, and variability in the same place from year to year, month to month, day to day and even hour to hour. In addition to variability, two other factors, cold and precipitation (especially snow fall), are predominant.

The coldest temperature ever recorded in Yellowstone National Park was 66 degrees below zero at the old Riverside Ranger Station on February 9, 1933. The warmest was 98 degrees at the Lamar Ranger Station on June 23, 1936. The difference between the two reporting stations: 164 degrees! Since the beginning of recording in Yellowstone in 1887, a temperature of 100 degrees has never been observed at any location inside the park.

Moderate summertime temperatures make Yellowstone's climate very agreeable—usually. Temperatures in the 70s are most common, but visitors should be prepared for anything that Yellowstone's variability can bring. Every reporting station in the park for example, has had snow at one time or another during every month of the year. On August 25, 1910 the mercury dipped to seven degrees at Lamar, the same station which reported the record-breaking 98 degrees in June, 1936. That a June temperature could exceed an August temperature by 91 degrees at the same location is remarkable indeed!

While winter temperatures in Yellowstone frequently dip below zero and lows of 40 below or colder are reached nearly every winter somewhere in the park, readings in the teens and 20s are probably most common. The community of West Yellowstone just beyond the western boundary of Yellowstone Park in Montana is often featured on national weather reports as the coldest spot in the nation, but Cooke City, Montana, just five miles beyond the northeast corner of Yellowstone is colder if one measures average yearly temperatures rather than only winter temperatures. By this standard, in fact, Cooke City is the coldest town in all of Montana.

The severity of winter snows in Yellowstone is largely a function of altitude where a few thousand feet difference in elevation can account for

Winter's a special drama in Yellowstone. PHOTO COURTESY OF YELLOWSTONE PARK CO.

double the accumulation of snow. Snow depth and water content are measured monthly at several sites, called snow courses, in Yellowstone and compiled by the Soil Conservation Service. Most snow courses in Yellowstone have been measured for the last 45 years or more. All of these are at relatively low elevations of between 7,000 and 8,000 feet except for one site near Cooke City at 8,150 feet. No regular measurements are taken at the higher elevations which account for much of the area of Yellowstone National Park, but snow pack at these locations is undoubtedly greater.

Federal weather officials, for example, have noted snow-pack depths of more than 150 inches above Heart Lake and seasonal snow-fall totals of more than 400 inches along areas of the eastern park boundary.

The soldiers who manned old Fort Yellowstone used to say that "in Yellowstone there are only two seasons, winter and July."

Below are the average snow depths as of April 1 for the years 1937-1981 at four Yellowstone Park snow courses and one nearby snow course above Cook City.

Average Snow Depths as of April 1
(1937-1981)

Snow Course	Elevation	Average Depth
Above Cooke City	8,150 ft	62"
Thumb Divide	7,950 ft	65"
Canyon	7,940 ft	50"
Norris Basin	7,500 ft	35"
Below Sylvan Pass	7,100 ft	45"

Highest and Lowest Accumulations as of April 1
(1966-1981)

Snow Course	Elevation	High	Low
Above Cooke City	8,150 ft	81" (1971)	41" (1966)
Thumb Divide	7,950 ft	111" (1943)	32" (1941 & 1977)
Canyon	7,940 ft	67" (1971)	27" (1941)
Norris Basin	7,500 ft	50" (1965)	23" (1940 & 1941)
Below Sylvan Pass	7,100 ft	71" (1960)	24" (1943)

Reading the Montana Skies

by Dorothy Stockton

███████ NORTHERN LIGHTS ███████

The real sky shows in Montana are the auroral displays. Montana is northerly enough to host a dozen or so a year. The clear skies literally become a gigantic television screen as electrons straight from the sun cause the oxygen and nitrogen to glow white, red, blue and green. The lights are actually the visible path of charged particles as they stream to earth outlining the shifting changes in the magnetic and electric fields of the sky.

Watching this display, you'll probably become caught in the excitement of finding each new splash of light. Your eyes constantly scan the skies searching for each new shimmer. And you shout! There really should be music, majestic music with drums but the skies are silent in their show. Even if your neck hurts from looking up, you keep on because you musn't miss such splendor.

One of the loveliest displays was August, 1978 in Helena. Hundreds of us were dancing in the streets, yelling and shouting in the middle of the night. The rays of light actually peaked over our heads so there were streaks in every direction—north, south, east and west.

Not all auroral displays are so spectacular. The most common are simple and quiet configurations which resemble the dawn skies. In fact, these are easy to miss because your first thought is that you're looking at an early sunrise. Then you realize the lights are north instead of east and that dawn is hours away. You are seeing an aurora. There is usually no color and no change, only a bright portion of sky near the horizon that fades into the night sky.

A slightly more intense display shows rays like vertical streaks, or "brush marks," of light. Watch these streaks develop as they scoot across the sky, sometimes with deep red hues. Each ray lasts only a few moments while new ones are constantly competing for your attention.

A really intense display superimposes dark rays upon light ones rather like curtains of light.

Each auroral display is unique, changing moment by moment. Even the same display appears quite different from each site.

Aurora are circular sheets of light that form a halo around the earth's geomagnetic poles. These geomagnetic poles are not the same as the earth's axis of rotation, called the North and South Poles. The magnetic poles change, but at the present time the northern one is off the northwestern tip of Greenland. The largest number of displays occur in an oval around this point, which makes Montana an excellent site.

Auroras start on the sun with a storm we call a flare. The flare sends a stream of electrically charged particles at less than the speed of light, but auroral displays remain unpredictable because that stream of particles must exactly intercept the earth across 93 million miles of space.

If the charged particles do intercept, the magnetic field which surrounds the earth accelerates and channels them into ribbon-like sheets which

Patterns in the sky: Most of us snooze through the midnight magic of Montaña's northern lights. PHOTO BY ROGER E. YOUNT, SR.

form a ring like a halo around both the North and South geomagnetic poles. The thickness varies from a few miles to a few hundred miles. That is, the aurora have a depth which can be measured. Usually, the greater the storm on the sun, the thicker the halo and the closer the halo moves toward the equator. The lights extend upward a few hundred miles and horizontally, a few thousand. Most displays occur during the equinox—March and September. I usually see five or 10 auroras a year here in Helena.

To further clarify this process, S.I. Akasofu of the University of Alaska writes: "The earth is surrounded by a gigantic magnetic field 'bubble' which protects us from most of the particles the sun sends out. During a solar storm, the particles compress this shield. On the other hand, the solar particles and the magnetic bubble make up a gigantic, invisible generator. The electric power generated by this natural generator is discharged through the polar upper atmosphere. The process is essentially the same as that of a neon sign, so that the aurora is a sort of natural neon sign. The power associated with the discharge would easily light up many New York Cities!

" . . . As the power of the generator increases, the ring-shaped region expands, sometimes down to the latitude of Helena. This tends to occur a few days after an intense solar flare. This is why the aurora can be seen at Helena rather than at higher latitudes."

Since I never want to miss an aurora, I set my alarm on clear nights. When I get up during the night, I check the north skies. If the display looks promising, I drive out into the country where the aurora is more defined in the absence of city lights. Quite often, I take other interested people as this is the Helena Astronomical Society's money maker. People pay several dollars in advance to be awakened in the middle of the night so they can see an aurora.

VENUS BY DAY

The clear skies of Montana present celestial splendors. Sometimes I have almost touched the stars. The skies were clear enough. I was just too short.

Even the daytime skies enhance viewing. One exhilarating summer day, I actually followed Venus across the sky from when it rose in the east until it set in the west in the afternoon. Although I had no binoculars or telescope, my freedom from obligations that day allowed me to check on Venus' progress. Each time I located it, I marked the spot in the sky by reference to a building or a tree. Fifteen minutes later, standing in exactly the same spot and starting with the previous site, I would move my eyes slightly west. Each re-discovery was a thrill because I had never read of anyone actually seeing Venus all day.

Of course, in my excitement, I was frequently pointing at the sky. And since nothing was easily visible, many people asked what I could possibly see. So I showed Venus to several hundred astonished people that day. Many had never realized they were looking at a planet, and *none* had ever seen Venus by day.

The technique is simple. Begin by locating Venus in the dark skies. If Venus is an evening "star," then try to locate it 15 minutes earlier each successive evening. If Venus is a morning "star," simply follow it as I did.

For only about a month each year is Venus brilliant enough to be seen in the daytime. Most astronomy calendars will give the date of Venus' greatest brilliancy. But in Montana, you can see Venus for several weeks on either side of that date. *See "Sky Calendar," East Lansing, Michigan 48424: Abrams Planetarium. $3.50/year.*

RAINBOWS & HALOS

Montana's clear skies also host outstanding rainbows. The colors are brilliant. Several times a year, the bow extends from horizon to horizon. One exceptionally bright rainbow I observed had a complete secondary bow. The secondary rainbow has the colors in reverse and is usually somewhat dimmer. But in this case, the secondary bow had vivid colors.

About a dozen times a year, Montanans see what appear to be patches of rainbows on either side of the sun. We call them sun dogs. Like rainbows, they are caused by moisture in the air which separates light into its various colors. Sun dogs differ from rainbows in two ways. First, they are located on either side as you look toward (never at) the sun, whereas the sun is to your back when you see a rainbow. Second, the moisture is in the form of ice crystals instead of water. All these ice crystals are the same size and shape. They even are falling in alignment. These crystals refract the sun's light in two patches both of which are 22 degrees on either side of the sun. The more brilliant the display, the more aligned are the crystals. And some "mock suns," as sun dogs are often called, can dazzle your eyes.

Halos are another phenomenon enhanced by the clear, cold Montana skies. They are caused by ice crystals high in cirrus clouds. Both the sun and moon may have halos—thin rings of light with a radius of either 22 degrees or 46 degrees. The 46 degree ring is relatively rare and fills half the sky.

But either size halo around the sun or moon has a reputation for signifying bad weather. Moist air moving before a storm is pushed high enough to freeze. The resulting ice crystals focus the light to form a ring. Unlike sun dogs, however, the crystals are tumbling unaligned which causes a ring. But the light is being refracted into its various colors and sometimes you can see an inner ring of red.

Ice crystals also cause columns of light above and below the source. Driving through eastern Montana one cold January evening, every car headlight and city streetlight displayed a brilliant column reaching high in the sky. The effect transformed ordinary towns into dazzling fairylands. And car headlights were visible from their columns long before the lights themselves crested the horizon. The next morning, the ice crystals formed a column above the rising sun. After the sun was high in the sky, the column was both above and below. Such clear columns indicate identical crystals falling in alignment.

HARVEST MOONS

I have come to look forward to full moons. Their light is perfect for skiing, sailing and swimming. But the autumn's full moons are special because they extend the day's length with an exceptionally bright light. The first full moon following the fall equinox is the Harvest Moon and the next is the Hunter's Moon. Instead of rising high above the horizon, these full moons skim the mountain tops. So we see them through twice the usual atmosphere. This gives them a special gold color and makes them appear gigantic. I always want to hold on to them—and some day I just may ride one!

SOLAR ECLIPSE

February 26, 1979, Montana was the ideal site for viewing a total solar eclipse. The moon's shadow fell right on our capital city. Although the eclipse itself lasted only a few minutes, our excitement began months earlier. Thousands of people chose Montana as their viewing site because of excellent chances for clear skies. We even had national TV broadcasting the event from atop a Helena hotel.

Disappointment dropped on sky watchers when we awakened to cloudy skies on E Day. Some people headed for eastern Montana in search of clear skies. Some of us were stuck here in Helena so we gathered in our pre-arranged places without much hope of seeing this once-in-a-lifetime event.

As eclipse time approached, we could see one hole in the clouds. I like to think our sheer will power and prayer had something to do with the fact that the hole revealed the sun at precisely the right moment. We saw the whole show!

The moon approached the sun's face and slowly slipped across. The skies grew darker and every living thing sensed the difference in the day. With the last flicker of sunlight, the moon's shadow swept over the land, momentarily silencing the crowds. Then we shouted. Some people set off firecrackers, others cried. Dogs began barking and howling nervously. We saw the flares on the sun at the moon's edge and the shimmering corona crowning the sun. Then, as suddenly as the eclipse started, the moon moved on.

The fear that clouds would spoil the event merely made our joy that much more intense. At least one person frantically paced several miles inside my living room afterwards as she repeated the same phrase, "I got to see the eclipse . . . I really got to see the eclipse." She was expressing the almost delirious excitement that many of us felt while experiencing night in the daytime.

EARLIER STUDENTS OF THE SKY

The Indians of Montana used the clear skies as their calendar. They observed that the sun rose at different places on the horizon at different times of the year. They did not know this was caused by the tilt of the earth's axis, but they did know how to use that information to make a calendar.

They constructed huge stone circles with straight lines extending beyond the extreme solar positions of June and December. By standing inside the circle and observing either the rising or setting sun, they could judge the approximate date.

I visited an Indian Medicine Wheel on the Sun River just before the June solstice. The sun actually did set exactly at sundown where indicated by the line of rocks placed several hundred years before by very astronomically astute people. Their sun dance, based on this calendar, probably would have been performed the next day.

Montana skies—they transform common sights into special shows. The stars, Venus, rainbows, sun dogs, halos, full moons and auroras keep us looking upward lest we miss the visual phenomena in our midst.

THE HUMAN ASPECT

It's Not a Drought 'Til It Breaks Your Heart

by Bruce Bair

Dryness in eastern Montana is more or less a normal condition that sometimes goes to extremes. Still, the statistics for the past few years have been brutal. Miles City's annual precipitation in 1979 was 8.68 inches, in 1980, 10.54 inches, and in the first four months of 1981, only .67 inches fell. The figures were similar over much of eastern Montana.

Dr. Ed Holroyd, a meteorologist with the government's Miles City cloud seeding experiment, has compiled and graphed rainfall statistics collected over the past 100 years and thinks that a dry cycle is just beginning, and the trend may continue into the '90s. He bases his opinion on a graph he constructed of the seven years' running average of precipitation, which shows moisture peaking about every 30 years. The peaks were during the 1910s, the 1940s and the 1970s. The valleys are in the 1900s, the 1930s and the 1960s.

A climatic study back to 1700 of tree rings conducted by the University of Arizona's Center for Tree Ring Research shows that drought periods in the West tend to recur and peak about every 20-plus years. This method of climate study predicts a drought beginning in the late 1970s and persisting into the 1980s. But tree ring studies also show there is no way to predict if a given year will be wet or dry, despite a trend, and so any year can be a wet one. The study also shows that the drought in the '30s was the most severe since 1700, making it unlikely a drought as unrelenting will occur soon.

• • •

When my mother remodeled our old farm house, the first thing she removed was the second story balcony. It was a wonderful place to play and dream you were sailing across the wheatfields on a ship, and though we loved it, it had to go for it was my father's lookout. He used it most frequently just before harvest, and would stride along it as he watched the

127

huge thunderheads forming in the west. Back and forth he would walk with worry on his face, and when the towering monsters approached his fields, which he could view from the balcony, he would curse at them as if he could turn them back with sheer vituperation. The hails came anyway, or didn't come, no matter how much he cursed. My mother counseled him to come to bed. "That doesn't do any good," she would say, but she couldn't prevent him from striding the balcony outside the bedroom window, sometimes until the early hours of the morning, until the storm had passed or broken up or had destroyed the wheat. She had the balcony removed so she could sleep.

I thought of it often, as I drove 10,000 miles of dirt roads in eastern Montana during the height of a drought. Those rainstorms of memory seemed so far away. Drought—it seeps into your soul as surely as the dust sifts inside the car. As I drove the empty 70 miles of gravel between Ekalaka and Alzada, the sheep pastures along the road were empty of animals, as barren as the seas of the moon. The only evidence of life was the saltbush, and the tiny craters left in the bare dirt by the hooves of the sheep. I remembered my father. He cursed drought, too.

"How can anyone live in a place like this? How can *anything* live?" I thought. I turned into a rancher's yard. The sheep had eaten everything, even the tufts of grass usually found along the foundations of the buildings. I knocked on the door and a balding man with three days' growth of whiskers answered. I explained my mission. "I'm the water rights man," I said. The rancher smiled ironically. "You see any water around here? Well, I guess we'll have to let you in." Then he asked the question everyone had asked for months. "Do you think it will ever rain?" "Always has," I replied. But I was not sure anymore. I had driven those roads from December through May, and not once had a drop of rain or a flake of snow hindered my progress. In January, I collected agates in my shirtsleeves in Prairie County, atop Big Sheep Mountain. It's hard to believe as I write this January. Outside it is 25 below, and there are two feet of snow on the level in Terry. The streets have slowly become plugged with it. The town is buried.

My answer to the rancher stuck in my throat. Perhaps it won't rain. Maybe eastern Montana is done for. Sometimes in self defense, I asked the question myself. "You think it will ever rain?" "No," some say flatly, "It can't rain." "Always has." But they were not sure. "What kind of question is that?" one asked. "Don't talk about it," said another gruffly. "Change the subject," said a ranch woman, waving the question away with her hands.

It was the same everywhere between Alzada and Ekalaka, and almost as bad everywhere else. No rain. The cattle had been sold months before. The sheep were living on imported alfalfa hay at $110 a ton. One rancher was lucky. He had 75 animals running on 25,000 acres. Spread out, the animals were easy prey for coyotes. The lambs thus abandoned were eaten by eagles. There was a narrow strip near Alzada that received above average rains, but only because, allowed the rancher, it rained seven inches in an hour. The accompanying hail killed a third of the sheep, stripped the grass to the roots, washed out the wheat fields and the reservoirs,

128

and accomplished in 10 minutes what generations of herbicide inventors could not—killed the sagebrush. "Even hailed out the hired man," said one of the grizzled veterans whose ranch was in the path of the storm.

"Ever seen such a danged dry place?" I had traveled every dirt road in four counties. "Yes, I think I have," I said. "Where?" the rancher demanded in disbelief. Few could imagine any place worse than where they were. I told him of the spot I found where the ranches claimed less than six inches of moisture in the past 19 months. That made him shake his head. "Hell," he said, "we've had eight." He looked around. The only green in 10 miles was his wife's house plants, which flourished in jungle-like profusion inside the windowed south porch. I counted him a lucky man.

Despite the worry in their eyes and at the corners of their mouths, there was not a single rancher who did not smile at least once at his own plight. Ranchers without humor do not suvive. "I don't know what we are going to do if it doesn't rain," they said, then they would smile. "Oh well, we'll manage somehow. Always have." They had watched the grass die back, the water holes dry up, the cattle culled to the best, and then the best sold off. Some sat in the middle of 50,000 acres with no animals but a favorite horse or two and a yard dog, and with nothing to do but clean out the reservoirs, fix the fences and hope for rain.

"Are you ruined? Can you get back in?" There was often a sly smile. "I've got enough tucked away to get back in if it ever rains. It's the danged *investors* who are in trouble. I've never had anything but cattle and 100 miles of fence. You don't get in trouble that way." When I walked through the rancher's yard, I saw that his pickup was a '57 model, with maybe a third of the original paint left. The bed was full of fence posts and wire. I had the feeling that rancher could weather 20 years of drought without stepping through the doors of a bank.

The dubious security of total self-reliance didn't prevent the ranchers from getting nervous on days when the clouds were scudding in the sky so furiously it *had* to rain. You could feel the lumps in their throats yourself, as they watched those clouds—when they heard the weatherman's predictions climb from 50 to 80 to 100 percent chances of rain. But bitterness clutched their hearts when the predictions failed. How could the weatherman be so wrong? They had watched those clouds gather so many times before, with the weatherman promising rain and the mindless disc jockeys broadcasting moisturous homilies.

It got so they just shut off the radio. They didn't listen to the weather. "Think it will rain?" "The weatherman says fifty percent," I answered. They shrugged. They had even stopped looking at the sky. They knew what no weatherman knows. That there is a principle of momentum that rules the weather, despite wet warm fronts and cold fronts and the collisions thereof. When it is dry, it tends to stay dry, and when it is wet, it tends to keep raining.

A rancher's wife summed it all up. "A drought isn't over until it breaks your heart. And it isn't a drought unless your heart is broken."

Direct Hit: Pilot Studies Lightning Close Up

by Lloyd Hansen

As a pilot for Johnson Flying Service in Missoula, I had the chance to see lightning in action at close range during flights for "Project Skyfire." One flight, in August 1968, brought the lightning too close for comfort.

The project was undertaken in the late 1960s and early 1970s by the U.S. Forest Service's Northern Forest Fire Laboratory in Missoula to investigate the actual sequence of events and physical factors involved in lightning-caused fires. Ground and airborne facilities were used to determine electrical and time-related characteristics of lightning strikes. Where possible, the site of the lightning strike was investigated on the ground to verify data gathered by the airborne and ground facilities.

Johnson Flying Service of Missoula, under contract to the Forest Service for a wide variety of flying services, provided the aircraft and crew for this research. The flying involved closely tracking selected thunderstorms within range of the ground station at the Missoula airport, gathering verifying data, and attempting to pinpoint the location of the lightning strike on the ground. The aircraft, a Cessna 206, was specially modified to accommodate the equipment needed to measure and record the electrical charges and duration of lightning strikes.

Flights were initiated when radar at Missoula showed that active thunderstorms would pass within range of the ground-based measuring equipment. A typical flight consisted of flying just beneath the base of the clouds, generally at about 7,000 feet, waiting for lightning to strike. When a discharge did occur, the equipment recorded the data while the crew attempted to locate the contact point on the ground and to determine if a fire had resulted. This initial finding was important because many, if not most, lightning fires are put out by the storm's own heavy rains.

Although strong turbulence may be expected when flying near thunderstorms, most flights were relatively smooth. But the flight that began on this August afternoon turned out not to be quite typical and resulted in spectacular, if minor, damage to the aircraft.

The summer had been hot and dry, too dry to spawn many thunderstorms, whose power depends on sun-heated, unstable, moist air. One of the very few isolated afternoon thunderstorms to come within range of the lightning recording station was cresting the Bitterroot Range to the south. The storm was exactly the sort of weather pilots are taught to avoid from their very first flying lesson, but our intention was to fly immediately under the most active portion of the storm. It wasn't very big by Great Plains standards, but any thunderstorm is dark and ominous if one intends to fly near it. Our storm slid down the east slope of Lolo Peak and headed northeast as we took off. Climbing toward the storm, I could see its dark underbelly churn as the storm grew not only in size but also in intensity. Sporadic lightning flashed from the east and south edges. In order to be able to identify the ground location of any lightning strike, we flew along these edges in an elliptical pattern perhaps eight miles long by two miles across.

The first rain crackled against the windscreen and wings like close-range gunfire, indicating the thunderstorm was fully mature. Six to eight miles above us the maelstrom was spinning, generating the multimillion-volt bolts we were seeking to understand. The rain stopped. The early rains in a thunderstorm are localized and intermittent. Several streaks of lightning tore the sky to the left, so we turned left and headed toward that area. The air had been surprisingly smooth, but it became progressively more turbulent as the storm grew.

Light airplanes, such as the Cessna we were flying, are quite noisy in flight so it is rare to hear an ouside noise. However, a peal of thunder from eight feet is impossible to miss. With a brilliant flash and an enormous bang, lightning struck the tail of the airplane. This was carrying the project of locating lightning strikes too far!

My first concern, after restarting my heart, was fire. No smoke was in the cockpit or trailing from the aircraft. Checking for structural damage, I exercised the flight and engine controls. They responded normally. I turned immediately toward the Missoula airport and began descending to land, still concerned about undiscovered structural damage.

I was definitely relieved as we touched down on the runway and taxied to the wet ramp. Mechanics immediately inspected the airplane. They found that lightning had struck the top of the left horizontal stabilizer about midspan, travelled through the metal structure of the airplane and exited at the tie-down ring on the bottom of the tail. The tie-down ring showed only superficial pits from arcing, while the top of the tail had a hole about the size of an orange burned through the skin. No other damage resulted from the event.

Flying continued on this project for the remainder of the season and for several more, but fortunately we never again had such a first-hand experience with the phenomena we were studying.

Weather
Sense and Nonsense

by Grayson Cordell

As early man emerged and began to support himself by hunting, fishing, planting and harvesting crops he began to have a need for knowledge of tomorrow's weather. He began to notice different phenomena that were at least occasionally followed by a specific type of weather. These observations were passed down from generation to generation and altered at times. Thus, weather lore has survived through the centuries.

Much of it is nonsensical and contradictory. But some does have a scientific basis. Many proverbs warn of rain if the sky is red.

> *Red in the morning   red at night*
> *sailors take warning;   sailor's delight.*

131

According to the Book of Matthew, Christ said:

*When it is evening, ye say it will be fair weather, for
the sky is red; and in the morning it will be foul
weather today, for the sky is red and lowering.*

Shakespeare wrote;

*A red morn, that ever yet betokened
Wreck to the seaman, tempest to the field
Sorrow to shepherds, woe unto the birds
Gust and foul flaws to herdmen and to birds.*

A red sky frequently indicates the presence of some of the elements
necessary for rain—moisture and dust. Of course, there are many other
factors involved also, but the sayings have merit. In the evening, when the
sun is in the west, red skies may indicate the storm has passed since
weather systems usually move from west to east in the middle latitudes in
which we live.

*Mare's tails and mackerel scales make tall ships
take in their sails.*

*Mackerel clouds in the sky,
Expect more wet than dry.*

*Mackerel sky,
Mackerel sky
Not long wet
And not long dry.*

The mackerel sky consists of rows of high, small, fleecy clouds that
often precede a warm front. Thus, there is logic to the proverbs, especially
if the clouds continue to thicken and merge into a continuous layer.

The following refers to building cumulus clouds of spring and summer
which often lead to showers or thunderstorms:

*When clouds appear
Like rocks and towers
The earth's refreshed
By frequent showers.*

Proverbs maintaining that rings around the sun or moon indicate pending rain or snow are frequently correct. The brighter the ring the greater
the chance of precipitation. The rings are caused by the light passing
through very high thin layers of clouds composed of ice crystals. These
clouds are often the advance clouds of an approaching storm.

*Halo around the sun or moon,
Rain or snow soon.*

The moon with a circle brings water in her beak.

A ring around the moon, rain comes soon.

Also true, if winds are light, are these proverbs which refer to clear nights.

> *Clear moon, frost soon.*
>
> *Moonlight nights have harder frosts.*

Numerous proverbs are based on the assumption that the moon controls the weather, but its effect is negligible. These are without any merit:

> *The bonnie moon is on her back, mend your shoes*
> *and sort your thack.*
>
> *Two moons in a calendar month bring a flood.*
>
> *New moon on its back indicates wind; standing on its*
> *points indicates rain in summer and snow in winter.*

The following proverbs, sound or not, are still entertaining:

> *Don't plant seed too soon, consult the moon.*
>
> *A wet fall indicates a cold and early winter.*
>
> *If the weather is fine, put on your cloak,*
> *If it is wet, do as you please.*
>
> *A windy May makes a fair year.*
>
> *Fish bite the least*
> *With wind in the east.*
>
> *When the wind is in the south,*
> *It blows the bait in the fishes' mouth.*
>
> *Rain by seven, stop by eleven.*
>
> *A warm Christmas, a cold Easter;*
> *A green Christmas, a white Easter.*

The big problem with weather proverbs is that they are not fitting in all locales. Sayings that are accurate in Europe are without basis in this country. In one location a wind from a specific direction brings fair weather, but a similar wind from the same direction brings rain in another locality.

> *Fair weather cometh out of the north.*
> (Book of Job)
>
> *The north wind bringeth forth rain.*
> (Book of Proverbs)

Certainly the mild and dry southwesterly chinook winds of the high Montana plains do not bring the same weather everywhere. Frequently they bring rain or snow to the western Montana mountains and valleys. The same southwest wind also is very wet in western Washington and Oregon. However, there, an east wind is dry, but an east wind on the Montana plains is frequently stormy. Thus, the location must be considered when using a proverb pertaining to wind direction.

A west wind carrieth water in his hand.

Rain from the east, two wet days at least.

When the wind is in the east,
Tis neither good for man nor beast.

When the wind is in the west,
the weather is always best.

A south wind in Montana frequently comes from the desert Southwest and is warm and dry even though it may later switch to southwest or west as a storm approaches the state. But in the southern Gulf States a south wind is humid and the wettest, stormiest weather comes from this direction. Sayings about south winds would not be valid in both Montana and the South.

When the wind's in the south,
The rain's in its mouth.

The south wind warms the aged.

The south wind is the father of the poor.

If feet swell, the change will be to the south,
and the same thing is a sign of a hurricane.

The southerly wind doth play the trumpet to his pur-
pose, and by his hollow whistling in the leaves
foretells a tempest and blustering sky.

Other lore just makes good sense. *"One would rather see a wolf in February than a peasant in his shirtsleeves"* means that very warm weather in February is unwelcome as it may start the growth of vegetation too early so that it is susceptible to later hard freezes.

A late spring never deceives.

A wet March makes a sad harvest.

Better be bitten by a snake than to feel the sun in
March.

A year of snow is a year of plenty.

February rain is only good to fill ditches.

And more—some worth noting, others not.

The rain does not fall on one roof alone.

The good rain, like a preacher does not know when to
stop.

A dry May and a dripping June,
Bringeth all things into tune.

A rainbow in the eastern sky,
The morrow will be fine and dry.

134

A rainbow in the west that gleams,
Rain tomorrow falls in streams.

Rainbow at noon, rain comes soon.

A little wind kindles, too much puts out the fire.

It is an ill wind that blows nobody any good.

No weather is ill if the wind be still.

When the stars begin to huddle,
the earth will soon become a puddle.

March comes in like a lion and goes out like a lamb.

Do business with men when the wind is in the
northwest.

The expression "it's raining cats and dogs" comes from northern mythology. The cat was supposed to have a great influence on the weather and the dog was a signal of wind. In old pictures from Germany the wind is often shown coming from the head of a dog. From this, the dog may be taken as a symbol of the wind that often accompanies a hard rain, while the cat symbolizes the rain itself.

The cock that ornaments many weather vanes originated in the ninth century. By papal enactment, a cock figure was set up on every church steeple as an emblem of Peter. This was in reference to his thrice denying Christ before the cock crowed twice. Thus, a "weathercock" is a person who is always changing his mind.

The temperature can be approximated closely by counting the chirps of a cricket. Count the number of chirps in 14 seconds and add 40. Three times out of four the number will be within one degree Fahrenheit of the air temperature.

Many proverbs are based upon one key day's weather as a sign of weather to come. Of course, one day's weather has no bearing on the future, but these sayings remain popular.

The most famous of these in this country is February 2, Ground Hog Day. In medieval Europe this was known as Candlemas Day.

If Candlemas Day be fair and bright,
Winter will have another flight;
But if Candlemas Day brings clouds and rain,
Winter is gone and won't come again.

Perhaps the most common key days in weather lore are Saints days. About 58 Saints days, in one land or another, are used to predict weather. One of the most widely known comes from England and is St. Swithin's Day, July 15.

St. Swithin's Day, if thou be fair,
For forty days 'twill rain no more,
St. Swithin's Day, if thou bring rain,
For forty days it will remain.

And also from England:

> *Before St. John's Day (June 24) for rain we pray,*
> *after that we get it anyway.*

Men have also seen signs of coming weather in the actions of animals and insects. Some examples are:

> *A bee was never caught in a shower.*

> *If the bees stay at home, rain will come soon,*
> *If they fly away, then fine is the day.*

> *Expect stormy weather when ants travel in lines,*
> *and fair weather when they scatter.*

> *When you hear the asses bray,*
> *We shall have rain on that day.*

> *If the cock crows before he goes to bed,*
> *He's sure to rise with a watery head.*

> *When flies congregate in swarms, rain follows soon.*

> *When harvest flies hum, there's warm weather to come.*

> *When sheep and lambs do gambol and fight,*
> *The weather will change before the night.*

> *Pigeons return home unusually early before rain.*

> *If the robin sings in the bush,*
> *Then the weather will be coarse;*
> *If the robin sings in the barn,*
> *The weather will be warm ...*

Of questionable meteorological value and without comment—

> *Dirty days hath September,*
> *April, June, and November;*
> *From January up to May*
> *The rain it raineth every day.*
> *All the rest have thirty-one*
> *Without a blessed gleam of sun;*
> *And if any of them had two and thirty,*
> *They'd be just as wet and twice as dirty.*

And finally—

> *Whether the weather be fine,*
> *Whether the weather be not,*
> *Whether the weather be cold,*
> *Whether the weather be hot,*
> *We'll weather the weather,*
> *Whatever the weather,*
> *Whether we like it or not ...*

136

Beyond the Comfort Range: Montana Record-Breakers

Compiled by Warren G. Harding

Temperature records:

Highest	117°, Glendive, July 20, 1893 117°, Medicine Lake, July 5, 1937
Lowest	-70°, Rogers Pass, January 20, 1954 (national record)
Greatest change in 24 hours	From 44° to -56°, Browning, January 23, 1916 (national record)
Most rapid change (7 min.)	From -32° to 15°, Great Falls, January 11, 1980, measured by thermograph (national record)

Precipitation records:

Greatest one hour	1.86 inches, Billings, July 2, 1958 (Actually fell in thirty minutes
Greatest 24 hours	11.50 inches, Circle, June 20, 1921
Greatest one year	55.51 inches, Summit, 1953
Least one year	2.97 inches, Belfry, 1960

Snowfall records:

Greatest 24 hours	44.0 inches, Summit, January 20, 1972
Greatest one storm	77.5 inches, Summit, January 17-22, 1972
Greatest one season	418.1 inches, Cooke City, 1977-1978

Wind record:

Fastest mile	82 m.p.h., Great Falls, December 10, 1956

Barometric pressure records:

Highest	1063.3 millibars or 31.40 inches, Helena, January 9, 1962
Lowest	975.3 millibars or 28.80 inches, Havre, January 11, 1932

It is often said that there is no normal weather, just extremes averaged into a normal. The saying has merit since our normal temperatures and normal precipitation amounts are an average of the extremes that occur each day. The extremes that are used for these averages are from records taken only where tested instruments with proper exposure are used. These are accepted as official recordings. Thus many record extremes occur where no certified instrumentation is available to make the recordings.

In the case of the fastest mile of wind recorded at Great Falls, it is an accepted fact that 82 m.p.h. for the fastest mile has been exceeded many times in the area from East Glacier to Browning and from Livingston to Big Timber. However, only National Weather Service stations compute the fastest mile, and there are none in these areas.

The effect of variations in exposure of an anemometer upon wind data can be illustrated by the fact that for many years the official anemometer for Great Falls was on the roof of the old administration building at the airport, and when the anemometer was moved down near the runways and located at the wing elevation of a jet aircraft ready for take-off, there was an immediate drop in the wind speed recorded of about twenty-five percent due to the lower exposure.

A CELSIUS/FARENHEIT COMPARISON

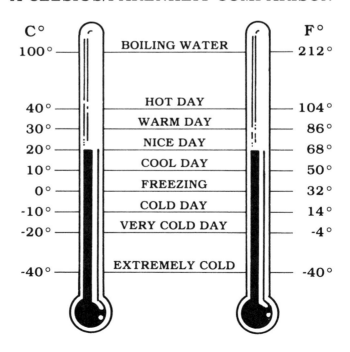

C°		F°
100°	BOILING WATER	212°
40°	HOT DAY	104°
30°	WARM DAY	86°
20°	NICE DAY	68°
10°	COOL DAY	50°
0°	FREEZING	32°
-10°	COLD DAY	14°
-20°	VERY COLD DAY	-4°
-40°	EXTREMELY COLD	-40°

Line of Duty: A Montana Veterinarian's Got Weather Woes

by Dr. Jack Ward

Duty hell! Just trying to make a living.

November 4, 1981 5 a.m. I'm on my way to the Big Hole for a day or two of hard work. Rain is crashing down in torrents as I drive south toward Lost Trail Pass. What appears to be a solid snowbank engulfs me as I gain elevation. Actually it's snowflakes, heavy, wet, the size of small envelopes. I gear down, dimming the lights for better vision to no avail; the wet snow has packed into the lights and diffused the beams. I stop to remove the snow, hands aching, fingers turning white with cold—not unusual in Montana after September 1! Fifty yards further and the headlights are again packed. Only one thing to do—roll down the window and watch the shoulder of the road, one hand on the wheel, the other over the defroster restoring circulation. As a large-animal veterinarian, I fight some unusual battles with Montana's inclement weather.

Meanwhile I've gained the summit of Lost Trail Pass. My eyes are aching with strain, my neck rigid with tension. It's time to pull over for a cup of coffee from my thermos. Revitalized, I inch on over Chief Joseph Pass. The snow has changed to fine, blowing powder, polishing the road to a treacherous glaze. I pull up at the ranch an hour later, greeted by a smiling, rosy-cheeked manager.

"Good morning, where have you been?"

I bite my lip and wonder what's so good about a morning that's zero degrees, with a 20 knot wind blowing snow down my neck and 600 cows to pregnancy test! Despite my sarcastic frame of mind, I manage a grim pleasantry, exhausted before the day's work has even begun. My hands are again throbbing with cold and I'm questioning my decision to become a veterinarian. Surely there's a warmer way to make a living!

• • •

March 8, 1965, 6:30 a.m. The phone rings. "Doc, I was out this morning and found four dead yearlings. Can you have a look?" John had purchased 300 head of yearlings about two weeks prior, so I suspected what the problem might be. I had moved to the Bitterroot after graduation from veterinary school because I'd been told it was the Banana Belt of Montana—always warm, hardly any wind. Well, somebody lied because as I stepped out of the house it was below zero and the wind was most definitely blowing. I clipped on down to Darby, pushing hard because I had other appointments lined up.

The calves were already frozen stiff so I performed most of the post mortems with an ax. After two or three autopsies and examining some sick calves, I diagnosed shipping fever complex. Treatment, prevention and care were prescribed. An hour behind now, I called my receptionist, Audrey, on the radio. She reported a colicky horse up the West Fork. I might as well take care of it now—I was running late anyway. The mare *was* colicky; after examination and sedation I gave her mineral oil, but the stomach tube was stiff as wire from the cold and had to be warmed up to prevent injury to the nasal sinus. Another hour behind, I headed back to the warmth of the office.

I was just getting comfortable when Audrey called to relay another message—an OB call from Ole Anderson who had purchased a place on the Bench Road. My emotions were mixed. Here was a new client, but at the same time the wind was blowing at 15 knots off El Capitan, 10 inches of snow had piled up, and the temperature was sinking. As I drove into the ranch I observed a cow in the middle of an otherwise empty 40-acre field. "I hope that isn't the one," I thought as I introduced myself. We climbed into the truck and sure enough the fellow directed me to the cow in the field.

My Swedish temper began to unwind from its hiding place. The hollow-eyed Hereford had been down so long she'd melted through 10 inches of snow and eight inches of frost, with a dead calf coming breech. An emergency indeed!

Returning to the truck, I prepared for the case by donning my short-sleeved rubber OB suit, which is basically worse than nothing. It's a very good conductor of heat and cold. The colder the weather, the colder the suit. The hotter the weather, the hotter the suit. I then lay on my stomach to examine the cow in 10 inches of blowing snow, a considerable part of which was going down the back of my neck. My temper approached boiling. Mr. Anderson, standing in a big sheepskin coat, wool pants, a Scotch cap with ear flaps down to his shoulders, speaks up and says, "Kinda vindy today." Wow! Have to hold my tongue.

"How long has this cow been down?"

"Oh, since a veek ago Sunday."

Considerable effort, some dissection, and 30 minutes later I had the fetus extracted. I was cold, saturated from a bath of urine the cow had bestowed down the unrepaired sleeve of my rubber suit. As I stood shivering, my teeth chattering, Mr. Anderson asked, "Are you cold?" Oh hell no!

Stripping to the skin and reclothing, I asked Mr. Anderson if he'd given the cow antibiotics. "Oh yah, about 30 cc's of penicillin a day for 10 days, but it hasn't helped." I stated that should be sufficient and hurried to get everything cleaned up, in the truck and gone before the cow passed beyond the great divide. Now three hours behind schedule, beginning to warm up, it occurred to me that I really didn't need new clients. Mr. Anderson had just convinced me.

February 13, 1966. The phone woke me at 6 a.m. "Doccy, another one of these heifers is in trouble." Walt Stewart always called me "Doccy" but after five years of practice I had become accustomed to all kinds of names. Walt had retired to a small place from a ranch in the Big Hole, and maintained a few cows. He had 10 first-calf heifers, and having little else to do, fed them generously—in fact, too much. This was the seventh to calve, and to date I had done four Caesarean sections and assisted the other two. As I left the house the thermometer read 23 below. I was cold before I started.

The heifer was inside an open Quonset hut, the best conductor of heat and cold I know, with the exception of my OB suit which I was again pull-

140

ing on. As I entered the building I felt all the cold in the country concentrated there.

I examined the heifer. Her calf was of considerable size, but I decided to try a normal delivery. The only warm places around were inside the heifer and the bucket of hot water Walt had supplied. Attempting to pull the fetus after attaching chains and head snare, I picked up my calf puller. My wet hands stuck to it like Super Glue. By pouring water over my hands, the metal calf puller came away quickly, removing only a couple of layers of skin. Unable to deliver the calf normally, a C-section was performed. It must be a total shock for a newborn to emerge from a temperature of approximately 100 degrees to 20 below. By the time the last suture was taken I was frozen, Walt was frozen, ice was forming on the pail of water and the calf's ears were beginning to freeze. Walt told me it was warm-up time and I didn't argue. I picked up the newborn and headed for the house.

Walt's wife, Pearl, met us at the door. She was accustomed to having a newborn, wet, slimy calf in the kitchen. Pearl poured us steaming cups of coffee, laced them with two or three ounces of bourbon and said matter-of-factly, "I've warmed Walter up many times." Thirty minutes later, toasty and mellow from the second shot of bourbon, I noticed the calf was attempting to get up on the slick kitchen floor, making a mess of things. It was time to get on with the day. I checked the heifer, cleaned my equipment and could have sworn it had warmed up 20 degrees. But it was no doubt my imagination and Pearl's good bourbon.

I have never again looked at the thermometer before heading out on a call. The psychological effect is too devastating.

July 4, 1969. This is a day of socializing for most folks—picnics, parades, rodeos. But for me it's a day of seclusion, out of the hot sun, sipping an iced drink and reacquainting myself with my family.

I was lounging on the patio when the phone rang. I answered. My mistake. "Doc, this is Dick. I was riding this morning and found a cow with vaginal prolapse."

"How long has it been out?"

"Don't know, but it's been a while."

Prolapse is an inherited weakness of Hereford cattle. The vagina inverts causing considerable problems and tending to reoccur after once happening. The common procedure is usually to cull these cows from a herd.

Hoping I might land an easy case, I drove 40 miles in 90 degree heat and was already beat by the time I pulled up at the corral. The sight awaiting me didn't lift my spirits. Here was an old, chronic prolapse the size of a basketball, sun-tanned and tougher that a Texas boot.

"Dick, I thought I told you to cull this cow a long time ago."

"Yes, I know Doc but she has a real good heifer calf and besides, I've got three good females in the herd out of her."

An hour later I had reduced the prolapse from the size of a basketball to the size of a baseball, ready to replace in the original position. Now the straining began. An epidural, or pain-killing shot, is supposed to help according to my college professors, but in these cases, it takes more perserverance and manpower to see who is the strongest—you or the cow. The drinks I had enjoyed at home began to pour through my skin in the rubber suit and in a few minutes I was wringing wet. She'd had so many epidurals already, the scar tissue was too thick to insert a needle through

141

easily. After five attempts everything was in place. The next problem was keeping it there while using the new prolapse pins for the first time. These are a special plastic device with sharp needles that hold everything in place while healing.

Sweating profusely, heated to profound misery, I stuck myself three times before the pins were placed. They poked out like a TV antenna through the top of the hips. I bobbed the cow's tail and both ears so she would be easy to spot in the fall.

"Dick, now you'll know her so you can get rid of her this fall."

"Damn, Doc, she's a good cow, a good producer, only seven years old and has a calf every year."

Oh yes. These kind always get pregnant, but at least I tried. See you again next year, cow number 123.

•   •   •

I have 24 years of practice in veterinary medicine to date. There's an old adage that states: "You have never practiced large-animal medicine until you have performed a Caesarean at 20 below or replaced a prolapse on the 4th of July." I guess I've qualified on both counts.

West Yellowstone Winter: Surviving It

by David Warner

Not all West Yellowstone "old-timers" are old. Membership in this honored and loyal order does not depend on a mere accumulation of years, but rather on the sharing of a number of singular experiences. And the most unique experience of all, the one most devotedly recalled and reminisced over, was that of surviving the winters in the town's early years.

West Yellowstone came into being at the turn of this century, when the Union Pacific Railroad completed a spur line north from Idaho Falls, Idaho, to a terminus on Yellowstone National Park's western border. Over the next several years many thousands of vacationing sightseers took what must have been a grand and regal holiday, riding the train from Salt Lake City to West Yellowstone, then travelling by coach and later by bus to view the park's many wonders. While it was possible in those first years to homestead and farm a piece of nearby land, West Yellowstone's existence has from the beginning depended surely and simply on the contents of a tourist's wallet, and economically speaking there has never been much of any other reason for the place to be where it is.

In those days a Yellowstone holiday was strictly a summertime affair. In the fall the trains stopped running and the travelers stopped coming. The "cabin camps"—Cro-Magnon motels—were closed, and so too the souvenir stores, cafes, dance halls and saloons. Inevitably the snow began to fall, usually in October. During the 1981-82 winter, something in the neighborhood of 20 feet fell, which most long-time observers agreed was

PHOTO BY RICK GRAETZ

fairly run-of-the-mill by today's standards. Everyone who has been around long enough to judge insists that there used to be much more snow. Psychologists claim that people generally exaggerate such things, that *everyone* believes the snow was deeper when they were young. When forced to choose between a psychologist and a person, however, I invariably side with the latter. The snow was a good deal deeper when I was a boy too.

Bob Smith tends a bar and guides hopeful fishermen. He tells his incredulous customers, "Today everybody's got a plow on their pickup. It didn't used to be like that. Years ago, when winter came this town just snowed up." And that is literally what happened; West Yellowstone filled with snow, every square inch of it. The city had no government and no snow removal equipment. State and county governments could not justify the expense of keeping the long-empty highways clear. So the snow fell and it stayed where it fell. Cars were parked in a grove of trees where they were soon buried and forgotten. The nearest town to the north was Bozeman 90 miles away. Ashton, Idaho was 65 miles to the south. There were no destinations in the other directions. West Yellowstone is one of the very few places in the world where the punch line "You can't get there from here" really applies. In winter no one could get anywhere from here. The inhabitants were in fact bound by snow, trussed up and locked up, with no resources whatever except their own. There were no tourists, no money coming in, no jobs, no traffic. There was no reason for the town to be, except of course for the most primal reason of all—it was a place where people had homes and families.

Some folks envied the geese and got out; but most couldn't and didn't. In the early '30s Ed Daley worked summers for a park concession. By the time his job was finished and battened down it was late fall. The first year he considered going to California. "But what would have been the use?" he says now. "To look for work? In the '30s?" Instead he stayed on, and "had the best winter of my whole life. Any silly thing you could think of to do, you had plenty of help."

The first consideration for those who stayed was a winter's stock of food, a grubstake they called it. Carrie Fuller "came into the country" when she was a little girl. Her family traveled from Pennsylvania to homestead. Her mother had long suffered from asthma and a doctor prescribed a higher, healthier climate. Mrs. Fuller remembers the family renting a small room when they got off the train. "My mother told us she felt so good she believed she could run. In all my life I'd never seen Mother even walk fast, and I told her, 'Oh, do it, Mom!' And she ran around in a circle in that room. I never saw anyone look so happy." The memory returns with remarkable clarity, considering the fact that her mother's indoor run took place over 70 years ago. Mrs. Fuller recalls the grubstakes. "We bought dried fruit in 25 pound sacks, and 100 pound sacks of flour. We figured on one sack a month and usually got eight, to be on the safe side."

Sis Staebler's family owned tourist cabins, and later she and her husband Roland ran a grocery store. They stocked up on potatoes, onions, cabbages, things that would keep in a root cellar. They bought case goods; she remembers lots of Jello; and also remembers that heads of lettuce, wrapped tightly in brown paper bags, would keep for a long time. The average cost of a family's stake was $100. Eggs and milk were raised locally and marketed house to house via horse-drawn toboggan. Wild meat was a staple. Bob Smith tells of a particular game warden who made certain every family had their winter meat. "He seemed to know that so and so hadn't gotten their elk yet, and he'd let on that he'd seen a nice fat one out by the river just that morning."

So the 50 or so households began the long dark months, with their cabins chinked tightly around them, their heat stacked in a woodpile by the back door, their food stored on shelves, holed away under the cabins, and hanging from a hook in an outdoor shed. There was no electricity, no running water. Pumps were primed each morning with stove-heated water. There was no doctor, and consequently or not, very little sickness. When people did have ailments they were tended by Mrs. Nellie Whitman, a reverentially remembered, kind and competent soul who read a "doctor book," kept a stock of carbolic acid, turpentine and chloroform, and possessed the caring to sit all night by the bedside of someone who needed her. With their physical needs thus provided for, the only other requirement, humans being naturally inquisitive, mobile, antsy animals was "Something To Do."

The children went to school in a two room building in the center of town. The graduates of this academy universally hold that they received a better education than do today's children in the newer, 40-room, brick building across the street. The original school's central location was fortuitous for reasons beyond the children's convenience. Because the youngsters were the only people in town who had to be someplace in the mornings, their paths were the only ones made, and in the natural course of things became the only paths at all. Consequently if one wished to travel from Point A to Point B, and one didn't feel like putting on skis and breaking a trail through the drifts, one walked from Point A to the school and then from the school to Point B. From the air the town must have looked like a giant wheel with a circle of spokes radiating from the school house hub. Bob Smith's home was on the edge of town, and on his way to school he went to the Hanson house across the "street" and met his classmates. He went into the house by the front door and then left with his friends out the back. As a result, the only way for anybody to get to and from the Smith residence was first to negotiate the entire length of the Hanson residence, from one end to the other. That was the sort of town it was, and those were the sort of winters they were.

Everyone, children and adults alike, skied. Approximately two miles from town, at the end of a long straightaway through the trees, was the Madison River and its steeply pitched banks. At one time soldiers patrolled the park on horseback and stables had been built in the vicinity. The Barns became the name of the favorite hill. Even today novice skiers are encouraged by local enthusiasts to go to The Barns, though all signs of equestrian activity and storage are long gone. Donna Spainhower, the current postmistress, speaks of weekends when nearly the entire population was skiing and picnicking along the river. She also remembers how she and her friends, living in essentially a flat city, improvised hills by sliding off roofs on the seats of several pairs of pants. The fact that such a sport was not suicidal attests to how deep the snow actually was, psychologists notwithstanding.

The skis were homemade; usually they were one-by-fours that were heated in a park hot pool and given the proper bend at one end. Tin cans were flattened for heel plates, and holes drilled for toe straps. Doughnut shaped pieces of inner tube were attached to the toe and then pulled tight around the heel. Poles were cut from willow clumps, and a small diameter tin can was slipped over one end, crimped down and nailed to the stick. Walt Stuart, present partriarch of one of the town's original families, tells of the waxes then in vogue, a personalized mixture of paraffin, coal tar, rosin, beeswax and Edison Records, all melted down, stirred together and painted on. The skis were extremely heavy and awkward things, compared to the fiberglass speedsters manufactured today. But no one realized the handicap under which they suffered and they skied anyway.

Bob Smith can recall only one boy who ever had a pair of store bought skis. "He was in hog heaven," Bob says. Otherwise such extravagances were unheard of. "We were poor in those days. Just one kid today has ten times more stuff than every kid put together back then. Of course, we didn't know it. It was just as normal then as the way we live now."

Except for brief instances of high adventure and passion, Bob's assessment is entirely correct. The "present" is so normal, so all-encompassing, that it is quite impossible to know which of its aspects will someday turn out to be special and memorable. Sometimes it is difficult indeed to imagine anything about the present time ever being recalled as particularly interesting or exciting. But if it is to happen, the first step would seem to be that the present must become the past—it has to be gone. It can be an interesting mental exercise: What everyday events and occurrences of the 1980s will we all someday look back on and swap stories about? Maybe at some future date every livable place in the world will be domed and climate-controlled, like a football field. Maybe someday a writer will sit across from me with his pad on his knee and ask what it used to be like.

"Well, son, I'll tell you. It sure is a lot different now. Why, years ago snow used to fall out of the sky, and come all the way down, right down to the buildings and concrete. I remember how we used to wake up in the mornings and have to plow it out of the way. Lord, those pickups were cold. We'd drive back and forth, pushing the stuff. It would take 15 or 20 minutes. It was hard work."

Such an exercise need not be humorous. What aspects of standard, old-hat 1980s reality will no longer exist in the 21st century? Internal combustion engines? Books? Mountain ranges? Bald eagles? Families? It is probably fortunate that we cannot know.

One of the favorite pastimes of many members of the adult community of West Yellowstone was Grocery Poker, a unique game that was played in the markets in the afternoons. One or two grocery stores managed to stay open through the winter, though the number of items available for purchase and the money with which to make such purchases both diminished at a steady rate as the months wore on. Credit was freely offered and freely taken. The people were neighbors, and trust and compassion were vital commodities. Entry to a store was gained in the manner of animals entering a common burrow—through a tunnel with an opening near the front door at a height approximately level with the building's eaves. Cal Fuller's Uncle Dave owned one such market. It was operated on a principle of self-service carried to the outermost limits. A shopper found what he needed, found a sack to put it in, and finally recorded the transaction in a credit book near the superfluous cash register. Neither Dave nor anyone else needed to be present.

Many forms of poker were actually played, but the stakes never changed. The gamblers played for credit at the store where the game took place. The dealing went on for hours. At the end of the day the details of winning and losing were worked out and recorded. Then the game began again the next afternoon. There was actually only one winter-long game, never really completed until the spring and a final, glorious reckoning. Sis Staebler remembers that her mother sometimes waited in line for a game to begin. "The games weren't that exciting, and no one really needed to win that desperately, but so many people felt if you didn't get a seat what in the world were you going to do for the rest of the day."

Sis's husband Roland had a pastime all his own. He shoveled snow. In a town where no one else ever did, Staebler, an unqualified monument to the notion of sticking to your guns, shoveled his driveway after every snowfall. When he had cleaned as far as the public street, he faced a wall of snow between 3 and 6 feet high. That didn't matter. Snow was to be shoveled. Staebler still shovels his driveway. He doesn't own a plow—not even a snowblower—and he shovels with a strength and steadiness well beyond the range of a typical 60 year old man. Last November Staebler turned 81.

The activity engaged in most often, with the most enthusiasm, was socializing. People visited, gave parties and dinners, played cards at each other's homes, held dances in the school. "Everybody was more sociable in those days," Carrie Fuller insists. "They really were."

Card parties were large-scale affairs, with several couples meeting at a house to eat and play 500. Things began in the early evening and at midnight "lunch" was served. The card playing then continued for the rest of the night until breakfast. Mrs. Staebler explains: "There was no work. No one had a job. There was no reason to get up in the morning, and so no reason to go to bed at night." Twenty-four hours of 500 were commonplace.

Dinner parties also involved the coming together of a number of families to share food and gossip. Small groups of people in a stringent environment, such as Eskimos or desert bedouins, tend to develop elaborate systems for sharing what little there is, and for making certain that the group as a whole comes through difficult times. Perhaps these dinners represented something of this basic human quality.

The school dances met the town's need for hoopla. Everyone attended. Families from outside town came by dog sled. Age was no barrier. Children came and babysat each other. The music was a homegrown blend of fiddle, piano and drum. Occasionally there were brightly decorated box lunches that were sold by auction at midnight. The men bid on a meal and then ate with the woman who made it. There was a constant stream of people in and out of the door. This was not because the revelers were unduly claustrophobic. The school in those days was the domain of a strong-minded, teetotaling custodian, and dance or no dance, he would not allow alcohol in his building. West Yellowstone was a hotbed of moonshining for many years; the lodgepole pines were thick and the stills hard to find. Now and then, as a means of quality control, the local residents would sample some of the product. The dances were a favorite occasion for such sampling, and knowing the custodian's prejudice, those with bottles would jam them into the snow banks along the paths outside the school door, fully intending of course to remember the cache's location as the night went along. The first several trips outside were satisfactory and rewarding, but dancing can be a strenuous activity and quite often late in the evening, overcome with fatigue, an owner would forget just where his container was stored. In the spring when the snow melted the front of the school resembled a dump for a cult of people devoted to a strict liquid diet.

The end of winter was marked by an extraordinary, Capistrano-like occurrence—the return of the trains. Every year near the end of March a locomotive with an enormous rotary plow attached to its snout began chewing its way east from Idaho, over the Continental Divide and into Montana and Yellowstone. When the 20-foot drifts had finally been breached, the train began its descent from the Divide with its whistle keening like a heralding bugle all the way into town. At the first hint of that long lost sound everything stopped. School was done for the day. Chores were forgotten. Everyone went to meet the train, and with it the rest of the world. Cal Fuller remembers the smell of fresh vegetables that the first train carried. Bob Smith remembers store bread. Donna Spainhower remembers bologna. The pioneer train was the reason for the biggest and grandest dance of all. Roland Staebler is sure the train crew deliberately arrived late in the day and then dallied getting the train turned around so that there wouldn't be time to return to Idaho and miss the celebration. Ed Daley says half the state of Idaho rode that train, looking forward to the gala in the evening. Bottles were lost by the case. It was spring.

Winter: Uncle Louie's Solution

by Loren Bahls

Lately there has surfaced in the northern latitudes of this country a coterie of hardy souls who indulge in a seasonal masochistic ritual known as winter recreation. Mostly stocky, robust specimens of Scandinavian ancestry, they look forward to winter with the same delight that Eric The Red must have felt the night before his first pillage of the British Isles.

The basic philosophy of these latter-day Norsemen in coping with winter is to ignore it. They continue their fair weather outdoor pursuits undaunted by ice, snow and sub-zero temperatures. Nothing is shunned. They jog, camp, picnic, canoe and hike long past the Fourth of July, a time when most sensible Montanans pack away their sweat socks, tent poles and picnic baskets for the long seige of winter that is widely known to emtomb the Treasure State for the better part of the year.

Folks in the uper Big Hole country call winter in Montana "The Hard Time," and with good reason. When temperatures drop to 70 below and the wind screams across the prairie at a hundred miles an hour, there is little thought of mint juleps and the easy life. Used to be Montanans endured untold hardships during the winter just to get by; now they do it for fun. Used to be, Montana's population relocated in Texas every winter. Now our winters are cherished lke a vintage bottle of chokecherry wine rediscovered after many years in the root cellar. And the longer and harder the winters, the better.

Not content with the more orthodox winter pastimes, Montana winterphiles have devised some really novel ways to suffer under the Big Sky. Take the Audubon Christmas Bird Count, for example. Any birder worth his seed knows there's a heck of a lot more birds around in June than in December, and it's a darn sight warmer too! And then there's the Late Gallatin Elk Hunt, when both the meat and the hunters go into the deep-freeze. The list is endless: dogsled races in Lincoln, ice fishing contests galore, and even a winter version of the venerable snipe hunt.

Survivors tell of solitude, lovely landscapes shrouded in snow, camaraderie around a warming fire, vigorous exercise and hearty appetites. What they don't recall, thanks to a blessedly short memory or perhaps a frozen cranium, are the chapped lips, runny noses, watery eyes, wet clothes and burnt fingers (from hastily grabbing the pot of stew hanging over that cozy warming fire).

My own aversion to winter began as a youngster in Minnesota, where frozen pump handles lurk around every corner and huge pointed icicles hang menacingly from every roof. If it wasn't the terrifying prospect of being skewered by a 20-pound icicle or losing a square inch of tongue-hide to a diabolic pump handle, it was the sheer boredom while waiting for the old junker to sink through the ice of Lake Winnehaha come spring thaw.

Perhaps the most colorful way ever devised to invoke suffering during any winter is the St. Paul Winter Carnival Grand Parade. As a cornet player in the high school band, I discovered that cornet mouth-pieces have the same thermo-metallurgical properties as pump handles and soon learned to stow my mouthpiece in my warmest pocket between painful renditions of "Our Director."

My Uncle Louie from Chinook had a better idea and fortunately he passed it along before his untimely demise last winter. Louie always maintained that the Hi-Line was a fine place to spend the winter, provided it was indoors. To really appreciate the stunning novelty of Uncle Louie's idea, one must consider the social climate in Chinook at the time.

Rumor has it that Chinook was settled during the last Ice Age by a tribe of Finlanders from North Dakota. As Montana's only town north of the Arctic Circle, Chinook quickly became The Mecca of wintermaniacs. (This was long before the invention of the snowmobile and West Yellowstone's rise to fame.)

Winter freaks converged on Chinook from as far away as Rudyard, Ingomar and Landusky to bask in the frigid glow at 40 below. The Chamber of Commerce made concerted efforts to dispel the rumor that Chinook was in any way associated with the weather phenomenon of the same name, claiming the last one blew by on August 15, 1893 and that the town has been under permafrost ever since.

City Fathers sponsored annual, actually perennial, winter follies and outdid themselves thinking up new events. One year the sun dog calling contest was really big. The next year the most popular events were the nightly Northern Lights shows, for which the local utility took all the credit. Even during the war years when electricity was rationed in Chinook there were many exciting events, like watching the Great Northern freight trains go by or listening to mosquito larvae through the ice of the Milk River. (If the wrigglers were audible above the din of a GN freight, it was bound to be a bad summer ahead!)

So Uncle Louie had his work cut out for him and his warm, sensible ideas were met with constant derision. Louie's innovation was not so much the indoor winter, but his rediscovery of the den.

When I was a youngster, a den was something proudly maintained by the eldest male member of every middle-class household. Wood panelled and minimally equipped with a fireplace, overstuffed chair and reading lamp, it was a place of refuge and comtemplation on long winter evenings, a place no more strenuous than turning the pages of a book or raising a cup of hot chocolate to your lips.

With the dawning of this very physical, exercise-conscious age, dens have quietly slipped into obscurity. If they are kept at all they are kept furtively or given other names—like library or study—names that do not connote the slovenly habit of just sitting, reflecting and keeping warm. More often than not, and at great expense to our collective psyches, dens have been converted to the likes of spare bedrooms, game rooms, family rooms, sewing rooms, plant rooms and music rooms, even though no one in the family can thread a needle or carry a tune.

Uncle Louie was a man of modest means and his house was small. Confined to their little bungalow as winter descended, Uncle Louie's already bad habits grew worse and Aunt Louise's already short temper grew even shorter. About November 15 every fall Uncle Louie was summarily banished to the cellar to commiserate with the stewed tomatoes and peach preserves. So it was here that he set up his den, a refuge from winter and woman. This proved to be his undoing.

He resurrected a pot-belly stove from the shed out back, dragged a splendid old leather-covered rocker down from the attic, and stocked up on snoose and back issues of the Farm Journal. Thus prepared, Uncle Louie could weather any winter the Hi-Line could muster, any winter, that is, until the last one.

Getting on in years, Louie liked his environment *warm*. One night he fired up his old wood burner until it was red hot. After a few complacent thoughts about this and that, Louie dozed off. On a shelf nearby was a coffee can full of popcorn, which soon began to do what popcorn does when it gets hot, engulfing Louie in a shower of white puffs. Nearsighted as he was, Uncle Louie woke up thinking he was caught in a blizzard, and promptly froze to death.

Winters are tough in Montana, even indoors.

A Recipe for Cough Syrup— And a Cure for Winter Blues!

by Merton Boyd

Quackery is a serious quasi-medical malpractice, whether by a licensed physician, a registered pharmacist or a well-intentioned but illicit herbalist. As a student and user of wild and cultivated herbs, I cannot claim without a potential lawsuit that the following economical and toothsome cough medicine will work for anyone except myself. Not to waste time, teetotalers may want to stop reading right now, for the recipe contains (drool, slurp, gulp, gasp, wheeze, smack) whiskey.

In the service of history, however, it is my bounden duty to record the recipe for this cough medicine. Surely it has already gone to Boot Hill early, with thousands of beneficiaries who gradually dispensed with the other ingredients. I myself now pen these lines not because I have one foot in the grave, but because only one of my hands remains out of it and I'm losing my grip.

William R. McCoy III, a friend, passed on the basic recipe to me in the finest tradition of oral history embellished with grunts and a slight slur, garnished with a hiccough and punctuated with a burp.

"You fill a jar with ripe chokecherries, but don't pack them in. Shake them so they stay loose. Unh. Then you pour in just as much sugar as the jar will hold. You keep capping and shaking the jar so the sugar will settle and you get in as much of it as possible. Unh. Then you slowly add just as much of your best bourbon as you can. Unh unh! All the sugar has to be dissolved with alcohol. . .every grain of it. Then you let it sit for a couple of weeks and it's ready, but the older it gets the better it is. And it doesn't take much. Unh. Just give kids three or four of the berries. You know. Have 'em eat the berries' flesh and suck on the pits for about. . .oh, ten minutes. . .and then they can spit 'em out. And it works."

"What's the adult dosage, Bill?" I wondered. "And can you drink the syrup?"

"Heh-heh."

This particular cough syrup recipe is probably not over two centuries old and is doubtless a Western adaptation of an older concoction. It has been in Bill's mother's side of the family since well back into the 1800s. It must be similar to the "Slavic booze" that poet Richard Hugo mentions, where in Washington a quantity of fruit was soaked in alcohol to flavor it further. I expect the fruit was eaten,too.

For a half-dozen reasons, I have experimented with several parts of the chokecherry bush, excepting the very young, reddish twigs which are reputed to be poisonous. The mature wood, inner bark, pits, and of course fruit are all useful for a variety of purposes.

Ripe chokecherries lose some of their mouth-puckering astringency if they are first frozen before use. Chokecherries picked previous to the first killer frost can be improved by a night in the deep freeze or freezer section of a refrigerator.

Preparing to make Montana Cough Medicine, I spread to dry a quantity of raw sugar purchased in a health food shop. This sugar is naturally brown from minerals and molasses, which have not been refined out of it.

At the state liquor store, my eager hands pounced upon a mickey of Early Times (this brand of bourbon felt like the appropriately symbolic choice). Since seeking a second medical opinion is in vogue, I also decided to make a batch of chokecherry cough syrup with Seagram's Seven Crown Whiskey, for it has unfailingly treated me well except for the 6,172 times I have mistreated it and gotten what I deserved. I made and set the two separate brands to "stew" in refrigerated, small jars on January 18, 1981.

About one month later, on February 16, to be exact, I entered into my ever-present notebook that my velar, vocal chords and throat began to itch and then burn. The inflamed, irritated tissue gave up much sputum, and I broke into a raspy, painful cough at regular intervals—every three to four minutes, as I timed the attacks.

After putting up for one-half hour with a rapidly worsening condition, at 5:05 p.m. I took one-quarter teaspoon of Montana Cough Medicine and I slowly chewed the flesh of four of the berries. I sucked on the chokecherry pits for 15 minutes before I spit them out.

In the half-hour that followed, I coughed only twice more. Then I took a nap until 7:25 p.m. Awakening, I had two coughing fits accompanied by the rise of a little sputum—a normal abnormality for a cigarette smoker—but the raw throat had gone away and did not return until 9 a.m. the next day, a 16-hour success for the medicine. By then I was teaching English classes at St. Joseph Elementary in Missoula . . . no place to take an alcoholic medication; and, it was after school before I could repeat the dosage. That time the cough went away for 14 hours.

I did not have to take the medicine a third time. The throat condition flared once on February 18 and then went away for good.

So I have used this chokecherry-flavored, Montana Cough Medicine only twice; but, when winter approaches once again, I'll be getting my feet wet and craftily leaving my hat at home, hoping to acquire a miserable chill. Colds were never in the least enjoyable until I discovered this remarkable cure!

The Authors

Loren Bahls is a free-lance writer and water quality specialist in Helena.

Bruce Bair is a free-lance writer residing in Terry. He has worked for several years on small newspapers and specializes in natural resource topics.

Merton Boyd is a columnist for the Missoulian and Montana Prospector Magazine. A Glasgow native, he teaches at St. Joseph Elementary in Missoula.

Mrs. Ruth Cameron is a free-lance writer whose articles have appeared in Persimmon Hill and Montana Magazine of Western History. Raised on a homestead north of Harlowton, she presently resides on a ranch near Martinsdale.

Grayson Cordell is the meteorologist-in-charge at the National Weather Service Office in Helena. He formerly served as state climatologist. His columns appear regularly in Montana Magazine.

Phillip E. Farnes is the Snow Survey Supervisor for the Montana USDA-Soil Conservation Service headquartered in Bozeman. He has specialized in mountain hydrology since 1954.

John W. Fassler resides in Great Falls. He has served as meteorologist-in-charge at Glasgow and as a state climatologist and hydrologist at Helena, in addition to several out-of-state posts.

Bob Frauson has been a park ranger for more than 30 years. The last 20 years he was Hudson Bay District Ranger in Glacier National Park until his retirement in April 1982. He now lives in the Columbia Falls area.

Donald M. Fuguay is project leader for forest fire meteorology at the Northern Forest Fire Laboratory in Missoula. He has conducted research for the Forest Service since 1958.

Dave Goens has been with the National Weather Service for 11 years. He resides in Missoula.

Lloyd Hansen is employed in Missoula by the Forest Service as a pilot flying retardant bombers, smokejumpers and parachute cargo.

Warren G. Harding is a meteorologist with Northwest Weather Associates, Inc., a Montana corporation based in Great Falls. A native of Havre, he began his career with the U.S. Weather Bureau in 1942. He recently retired from a position as lead forecaster at the National Weather Service state forecast center at Great Falls. He was awarded the Department of Commerce bronze medal for his research in the prediction of winter storms in Montana. His wife, Grace, a native of Simms, whose articles also appear in this book, trained at the weather school in Seattle, before accompanying Harding to Alaska where they served as Rawinsonde (upper air sounding) specialists for four years. They operate a ranch at Simms.

John G. Lepley is curator of the Ft. Benton Museum. A biology teacher for 29 years, he has also authored several articles for Montana the Magazine of Western History. His book, Luxury Living on the Levee, features old homes of Ft. Benton.

Tom Livers is an information officer with the Energy Division, Montana Department of Natural Resources and Conservation.

James E. Lotan is a research forester and program manager of the Fire Effects and Use Research and Development Program at the Northern Forest Fire Laboratory in Missoula. He has more than 20 years experience in forest research in Montana.

George D. Mueller, a native of Lewistown, was employed by the National Weather Service for nearly 27 years at Meacham, Oregon and Great Falls. Now retired, he researches and writes central Montana history.

152

William A. Rammer is a meteorologist with Northwest Weather Associates, Inc. in Great Falls. He served as meteorologist-in-charge at the state forecast center before retiring in 1981. In addition, he received the Department of Commerce Silver Medal for his work at the National Meteorological Center in Maryland.

Rick Reese is director of the Yellowstone Institute which conducts field seminars in Yellowstone National Park. He has authored numerous articles about Montana and the West.

Dorothy Stockton is a teacher at Helena Junior High. She offers astronomy workshops and classes for kindergarten through college.

Dick Thoroughman is a native of Ft. Shaw. He is a member of the Cascade County Historical Society, the Civil War Historical Society, the Sons of the Confederate Veterans and the Sons and Daughters of the Montana Pioneers. Currently he is employed by Cascade County.

Dr. Jack Ward, a native of Hysham, is a veterinarian specializing in equine and bovine practice in Hamilton. In addition to numerous research projects, he has authored several articles and presented lectures and seminars.

David Warner is a free-lance writer who has lived in West Yellowstone for seven years. He is a weather observer for the National Weather Service.

Glossary of Weather Terms

advection & convection—regarding the general distinction (in meteorology) between advection and convection, the former describes the predominantly horizontal, large-scale motions of the atmosphere while convection describes the predominantly vertical, locally induced motions.

almanac—a calendar to which astronomical and other data (often weather predictions) are commonly added. The word is of Arabic origin, meaning originally a camp or settlement (a place where camels kneel), and subsequently the weather at that place. It is now the Arabic word for weather.

anemometer—a device used to measure wind speed.

atmospheric pressure—(also called barometric pressure) the pressure exerted by the atmosphere as a consequence of gravitational attraction exerted upon the "column" of air lying directly above the point in question.

barogram—the continuous record made from a self-registering barometer.

blizzard—a severe weather condition characterized by low temperatures and by strong winds bearing a great amount of snow (mostly fine, dry snow picked up from the ground). The U.S. Weather Bureau specifies . . . a wind of 32 m.p.h. or higher, low temperatures, and sufficient snow in the air to reduce visibility to less than 500 feet; and for severe blizzard, wind speeds exceeding 45 m.p.h., temperatures near or below 10 degrees F., and visibility reduced by snow to near zero.

Celsius-Centigrade—a thermometer invented by the Swedish astronomer, Anders Celsius; 0 degrees denotes the temperature of melting ice and 100 degrees the temperature of boiling water, both under standard atmospheric pressure.

climate—the prevalent or characteristic meteorological conditions of a place or region.

climatologist—seeks to describe and explain the nature of climate, a result of weather, how it differs from place to place, and how it is related to man's activities.

cold front—the discontinuity at the forward edge of an advancing cold air mass which is displacing warmer air in its path.

downwind—the direction toward which the wind is blowing; with the wind.

easterly, westerly, etc.—direction from which the wind is blowing or from which a weather system is moving.

Fahrenheit—a thermometer where 32 degrees denotes the temperature of melting ice and 212 degrees the temperature of boiling water, both under standard atmospheric pressure.

fastest mile—over a specified period (usually the 24-hour observational day), the fastest speed in miles per hour, of any "mile" of wind. The accompanying direction is specified also. This record is maintained only at weather stations which have a multiple register, and thus have a time-record of the passing of each mile of wind. Could be compared to "peak gust."

Great Basin—area of southwestern U.S. mainly Utah and Nevada over which the semi-permanent basin high is located.

high pressure system—an area on the surface of high barometric pressure. Winds tend to blow clockwise and out of the system.

hydrometeor—a generic term for weather phenomena such as rain, cloud, fog etc., which mostly depend upon modifications in the condition of the water vapor in the atmosphere.

Indian summer—a period, in mid or late autumn, of abnormally warm weather, generally clear skies, sunny but hazy days, and cool nights . . . It does not occur every year; and in some years there may be two or three Indian summers. The term is most often heard in the northeastern United States, but its usage extends throughout English-speaking countries. It dates back at least to 1778, but its origin is not certain; the most probable suggestions relate it to the way the American Indians availed themselves of this extra opportunity to increase their winter stores. The comparable period in Europe is termed the "Old Wives' Summer," and poetically, may be referred to as "halcyon days." In England, dependent upon dates.

infra-red sensors—instruments capable of detecting temperatures of an object. When used with camera equipment a picture of the heat field is obtained.

inversion—an abbreviation for "inversion of the vertical gradient of temperature." The temperature of the air is ordinarily observed to become lower with increasing height, but occasionally the reverse is the case, and when the temperature increases with height, there is said to be an "inversion."

lee—the side or quarter away from the direction from which the wind blows; the side sheltered from the wind.

lightning stroke—any one of a series of repeated electrical discharges comprising a single lightning flash; specifically, in the case of the cloud-to-ground-discharge, a leader plus its subsequent return streamer.

low pressure system—an area on the surface of low barometric pressure. Winds tend to blow counterclockwise and towards the center of the system.

mean—average.

mean sea level—the average height of the sea surface, based upon hourly observation of tide height on the open coast or in adjacent waters which have free access to the sea. In the United States, mean sea level is defined as the average height of the surface of the sea for all stages of the tide over a nineteen-year period.

microclimate—the fine climatic structure of the air space which extends from the very surface of the earth to a height where the effects of the immediate character of the underlying surface no longer can be distinguished from the general local climate . . . generally, four times the height of surface growth or structures defines the level where microclimatic overtones disappear . . . (observe the microclimate of a putting green versus that of a redwood forest). Currently, the most studied broad types are: the "urban microclimate," affected by pavement, buildings, air pollution, dense inhabitation, etc.; the "vegetation microclimate," concerned with the complex nature of the air space occupied by vegetation and its effects upon the vegetation; and the microclimate of confined spaces of houses, greenhouses, caves, etc.

mirage—simple mirages may be any one of the three types, the "inferior mirage," the "superior mirage," or the "lateral mirage," depending, respectively, on whether the spurious image appears below, above, or to one side of the true position of the object. Of the three, the inferior mirage is the most common, being usually discernible over any heated street in daytime during summer. The abnormal refraction responsibile for mirages is invariably associated with abnormal temperature distributions that yield abnormal spatial variations.

National Weather Service—the public weather arm of the United States Government. It provides weather forecasts to the general public; issues warnings for tornadoes, floods, tsunamis (tidal waves), hurricanes, and other atmospheric and hydrologic hazards.

orographic—terrain influence on weather systems.

oscillation—generally, the process of varying above and below a mean value; usually a periodic process. (Compare fluctuation, cycle, wave.)

radiosonde, rasonde, rawinsonde—upper air soundings. First instruments only transmitted temperature, pressure, and relative humidity and were named radiosonde or rasonde. When tracking devices were developed to obtain a slant range on the instrument, wind data became available and the process was then called rawinsonde.

rain shadow—the region on the lee side of a mountain or mountain range, where the precipitation is noticeably less than on the windward side. A good example of rain shadow in the U.S. is the region east of the Sierra Nevadas; there the prevailing westerly winds deposit most of their moisture on the western slopes of the range.

snow shed—a protective structure erected over railroad tracks to prevent snow accumulation on the tracks. It is used where plowing is difficult, as in deep cuts, or where snow slides are frequent.

stratosphere—the upper regions of the atmosphere, in which the temperature is quite constant in the vertical.

surface trough—an elongated low pressure system on the surface.

thermograph—a recording thermometer which gives a continuous permanent record.

tropopause—the boundary between the lower atmosphere or troposphere and the stratosphere. Point at which the temperature ceases to decrease with altitude.

The tropopause averages from 6 to 9 miles in height, is lower over the poles and higher over the tropics. It is lower over a given area in winter than in summer. Very little moisture is found above the tropopause.

upper trough—an upper weather system or disturbance.

warm front—the discontinuity at the forward edge of an advancing warm air mass which is displacing a retreating colder air mass.

Genuine Montana Weather Rock

PLACE UNIT
OUTSIDE AND OBSERVE FOLLOWING:

1. If rock is wet, it's raining
2. If rock is white, it's snowing
3. If rock is moving back and forth, it's windy
4. If rock is hard to see, it's foggy
5. If rock is casting a shadow, it's sunny
6. If rock is cold, it's cold out.

This Montana Weather Rock never fails!